STRATEGIC

LEARNING

TECHNOLOGY

LEADERSHIP

STRATEGIC LEARNING TECHNOLOGY LEADERSHIP

STRATEGIZE LEARNING TECHNOLOGIES TO SPEED UP EMPLOYEE DEVELOPMENT IN THE ERA OF AI

Raman K. Attri, Dr

A Publication of Speed To Proficiency Research: S2Pro©

Copyrights © 2025 Raman K Attri and Speed To Proficiency Research: S2Pro©

All rights reserved. No part of this publication may be reproduced, distributed, or transmitted in any form or by any means, including photocopying, recording, or other electronic or mechanical methods, without the prior written permission of the author and publisher, except in the case of brief quotations embodied in critical reviews and certain other noncommercial uses permitted by copyright law.

ISBN: 978-981-18-7315-7 (e-book)
ISBN: 978-981-18-7313-3 (paperback)
ISBN: 978-981-18-7314-0 (hardcover)

Published in Singapore
Printed in the United States of America, Australia, the United Kingdom

https://www.speedtoproficiency.com
info@speedtoproficiency.com

National Library Board, Singapore Cataloguing in Publication Data

Name(s): Attri, Raman K., 1973-
Title: Strategic learning technology leadership : strategize learning technologies to speed up employee development in the era of AI / Raman K. Attri, Dr.
Description: Singapore : Speed To Proficiency Research, [2025]
Identifier(s): ISBN 978-981-18-7314-0 (hardcover) | ISBN 978-981-18-7313-3 (paperback) | ISBN 978-981-18-7315-7 (ebook)
Subject(s): LCSH: Business enterprises--Technological innovations. | Management--Technological innovations. | Technological innovations--Management. | Industrial management.
Classification: DDC 658.4--dc23

Acknowledgments:
Review: Abhinandan Mookherjee
Editing: Anupama Ganesh

To Rakesh Puril, a trusted friend, a motivator, and a cheerleader during challenging times of my life

PREFACE

In 2018, I embarked on a groundbreaking study that would transform how organizations approached employee development. I interviewed 85 world-class leaders and collected 66 project cases from over 70 world-class learning organizations in 42 industries. The study participants came from different business segments, job types, and skills, providing me with a broad range of contexts and settings for my research.

My goal was to explore how organizations could accelerate the proficiency curve and shorten time-to-proficiency. The findings from my research uncovered powerful insights into how organizations could achieve this goal.

Interestingly, alongside the main findings, I also discovered that these organizations implemented technologies and analytics strategically. I observed and studied approximately 200 different technologies that were used at various points of time during an employee's journey, starting from hiring to proficiency, as critical practices to shorten time-to-proficiency.

I also recognized the way such organizations made technological decisions that set them apart. That also meant that on a larger canvas, most other organizations lacked the culture or practice to establish strategic technologies focused on the 'speed' of employee development. Instead, they implemented technologies to improve employee learning, process efficiency, and resource efficiency, which were not enough to offer a competitive edge in the long run.

However, the COVID-19 pandemic changed everything. Traditional technologies failed to support the speed of skill acquisition and employee development, leaving many organizations struggling to cope with unforeseen situations. Only a handful of organizations with the right 'speed-savvy' culture could thrive and stay ahead of the competition.

This pandemic has opened the eyes of most learning technology executives to the need to rethink their technology strategy. Coupled with the challenges of remote and hybrid working at the onset of Industry 4.0 and the highly accelerated digital revolution, it is now understood that if organizations are to stay ahead of the curve, they need to diligently think about the speed of employee development.

As I revamped my research in the context of the challenges faced by leaders during the pandemic, I found my research to be more and more applicable in the era of speed. Organizations now need robust learning and HR technologies and a whole range of analytics that can be strategized in such a way as to support a sustainable speed over the competition. Ironically, most learning technologists, HR leaders, and corporate IT leaders are not trained on a leadership framework of 'speed' for faster development of employee skills and to prepare them for the era of speed.

In this book, I shall share a framework to polish your technology leadership through some breakthrough strategies based on my research and the implementations I drove during the pandemic technological revolution. Based on two decades of international research, over 25 years of corporate learning leadership, and authorship of 50 books, this revolutionary book distills first-hand, research-based wisdom from over 66 project case studies.

You will learn how organizations thinking futuristically have leveraged state-of-the-art technologies, analytics, tools, and systems to shorten the time-to-proficiency of their workforce and teams at the speed of business. You will learn to strategically leverage five types of analytics and five types of workplace technologies to develop workforce capabilities at the pace of business. You will acquire renewed business acumen from marrying workforce analytics, workplace technologies, and time-to-proficiency metrics. This integration allows building people analytics and learning technology strategies to improve employee performance faster.

You will learn five steps of institutionalizing, measuring, monitoring, tracking, and improving 'time-to-proficiency' metrics as an anchor before implementing expensive analytics platforms and new technologies for learning, HR, and employee performance.

I focus on developing you as a *strategic learning technology leader* who can revolutionize the organizational technology decision-making processes and positively contribute toward accelerating employee mastery to support business challenges.

Let's get there faster together!

Dr Raman K Attri

January 2025

CONTENTS

1
DIGITAL REVOLUTION IN LEARNING TECHNOLOGIES

DIGITAL LEARNING TECHNOLOGY REVOLUTION	3
TAKING IT FORWARD	13

2
BUSINESS KPIs FOR LEARNING TECHNOLOGIES

BUSINESS LANDSCAPE	19
THE TECHNOLOGY ROI TRAP	22
MEASURING EMPLOYEE DEVELOPMENT	25
KNOWING TTP METRICS	30
MARKET PRESSURES FOR SPEED	32
BENEFITS OF SHORTENING TTP	37
TAKING IT FORWARD	40

3
STRATEGIC LEARNING TECHNOLOGY LEADERSHIP THINKING

KEEPING HUMANS AT THE CENTER	47
FLAWS IN TRADITIONAL TECHNOLOGY DECISIONS	49

STRATEGIC LEARNING TECHNOLOGY LEADERSHIP FRAMEWORK	55
COMPETENCIES FOR STRATEGIC LEARNING TECHNOLOGY LEADERSHIP	72
TAKING IT FORWARD	75

4
TECHNOLOGIES & ANALYTICS FOR HIRING RIGHT

LOOK BEYOND BASIC DATA	81
TECHNOLOGIES FOR PERFORMER PROFILING	82
TAKING IT FORWARD	95

5
TECHNOLOGIES & ANALYTICS FOR PROFICIENCY METRICS

THRESHOLD PROFICIENCY METRICS	101
DECIDING THE PROFICIENCY MEASUREMENT APPROACH	108
TECHNOLOGIES AND ANALYTICS	109
TAKING IT FORWARD	112

6
TECHNOLOGIES & ANALYTICS FOR WORK SKILLS

WORK-SKILLS ANALYSIS	119
WORK-SKILLS ANALYTICS TECHNOLOGIES	120
TAKING IT FORWARD	125

7
TECHNOLOGIES & ANALYTICS FOR EFFICIENT LEARNING PATH

TECHNOLOGIES FOR EFFICIENT LEARNING PATHS	131
TECHNOLOGIES AND ANALYTICS	133
ADAPTIVE LEARNING PATH	135
TAKING IT FORWARD	138

8
TECHNOLOGIES & ANALYTICS FOR TIME MEASUREMENTS

TIME-TO-ACTIVITY VS TTP	145
STRATEGIC STANCE ON TIME MEASUREMENT	149
TAKING IT FORWARD	152

9
EMERGING TECHNOLOGIES FOR SPEED

THREE TYPES OF WORKFORCE ANALYTICS	160
FIVE TYPES OF LEARNING TECHNOLOGIES	167
EIGHT TYPES OF PERFORMANCE SUPPORT SYSTEMS	177
FOUR TYPES OF SOCIAL TECHNOLOGIES	190
AI-BASED E-LEARNING PLATFORMS AND TOOLS	198

10
FINAL THOUGHTS

TAKING IT FORWARD	209

11
MODELING GEN-AI FOR ENTERPRISE L&D

CONSUMER GEN-AI APPLIED TO L&D	217
SHOWCASING ENTERPRISE L&D WITH GEN-AI	219
SCALING UP CONSUMER GEN-AI	237
GEN-AI FOR ENTERPRISE DOCUMENTATION	239
KEEPING A FEW THINGS IN MIND	242
READERS' LEARNING RESOURCES	244

L&D CAREER RESOURCES

POWER-PACKED L&D BOOKS	249
TRAINING COURSES	251
SCIENCE OF SPEED IN L&D	252

BIBLIOGRAPHY

INDEX

ABBREVIATIONS

AI	Artificial intelligence
AR	Augmented reality
BI	Business intelligence
CCMS	Component Content Management Systems
CoP	Communities of Practice
CRM	Customer relationship management
CXO	Chief Executives
ERP	Employee resource processing
GEN AI	Generative Artificial Intelligence
IoT	Internet of Things
JIT	Just-in-time
KPI	Key performance indicators
L&D	Learning and Development
LMS	Learning management systems
ML	Machine learning
MR	Mixed Reality
MTTR	Mean time to repair
NLP	Natural language processing
PSS	Performance support systems
ROE	Return on Expectations
ROI	Return on Investment
SME	Subject matter experts
SOP	Standard operating procedure
TTP	Time-to-proficiency
VR	Virtual reality

Chapter 1
DIGITAL REVOLUTION IN LEARNING TECHNOLOGIES

Chapter 2
BUSINESS KPIs FOR LEARNING TECHNOLOGY

Chapter 3
STRATEGIC LEARNING TECHNOLOGY LEADERSHIP THINKING

Chapter 4
TECHNOLOGIES & ANALYTICS FOR HIRING RIGHT

Chapter 5
TECHNOLOGIES & ANALYTICS FOR PROFICIENCY METRICS

Chapter 6
TECHNOLOGIES & ANALYTICS FOR WORK SKILLS

Chapter 7
TECHNOLOGIES & ANALYTICS FOR EFFICIENT LEARNING PATH

Chapter 8
TECHNOLOGIES & ANALYTICS FOR TIME MEASUREMENTS

Chapter 9
EMERGING TECHNOLOGIES FOR SPEED

Chapter 10
THE FINAL THOUGHTS

BONUS
MODELLING GEN-AI FOR ENTERPRSE L&D

L&D CAREER RESOURCES

1
DIGITAL REVOLUTION IN LEARNING TECHNOLOGIES

1/ DIGITAL REVOLUTION IN LEARNING TECHNOLOGIES

The scope of learning technologies encompasses a wide range of tools, platforms, software, and systems that support acquiring and developing learners' knowledge and skills in various contexts. Learning technologies can be broadly defined as those used to support teaching, learning, or assessment. Thus, learning technologies are far broader in their applications, spanning a range of aspects such as employee learning, training, performance, certification, compliance, skill assessment, career progression, performance improvement and support, coaching and mentoring, documentation, and corporate knowledge access. These technologies also include related terms such as learning analytics, talent or people analytics, performance support systems (PSSs), and HR technologies.

DIGITAL LEARNING TECHNOLOGY REVOLUTION

Over the past two decades, the education and, training and learning industries have seen a significant shift in how they deliver and consume learning. Advancements in technology have brought in new tools and approaches that have enhanced the learning experience for students, making learning more engaging, interactive, and accessible. As we see back, elearning and learning technologies seem to have passed through three distinct phases:

2000-2010: Emergence of online learning

The first decade of the 21st century witnessed a significant shift toward online learning. The Internet was becoming widely available, which brought in new possibilities for learning. Online learning was seen as a way to provide access to education for those who could not attend traditional schools or universities. Soon, learning technologies were an integral part of corporate learning infrastructure.

Virtual classrooms

Virtual classrooms emerged as a significant development in online learning during this decade. Elluminate (1997), now known as Blackboard Collaborate, was one of the first virtual classroom tools. A virtual classroom is an online environment that mimics the traditional classroom setting, allowing students to interact with their peers and instructors in real time. This approach allows students to attend classes from anywhere, as long as they have an Internet connection. The virtual classroom also allows students to participate in discussions, ask questions, and collaborate on projects.

Learning management systems (LMSs)

Another significant development during this decade was the emergence of LMSs. WebCT (1996), now owned by Blackboard, was one of the first LMSs. An LMS is a software application used for the administration, documentation, tracking, reporting, and delivery of educational courses, training programs, or learning and development programs. LMSs have made the delivery of online courses, student progress management, and student performance tracking possible for educational institutions and organizations.

Web 2.0-based learning platforms

In the mid-2000s, the emergence of Web 2.0 technologies led to the development of new e-learning tools and platforms that allowed for more interactive and collaborative learning experiences. One such platform was Moodle, an open-source LMS, first released in 2002. Moodle allowed learning designers to create online courses effortlessly and provided various communication, collaboration, and assessment tools.

1/ DIGITAL REVOLUTION IN LEARNING TECHNOLOGIES

2010-2019: Rise of digital learning

The second decade of the 21st century saw a significant rise in mobile learning. With the proliferation of smartphones and tablets, learners can access learning materials anywhere and anytime. The rise of mobile learning also led to the development of new learning tools and platforms, such as apps, games, and simulations.

Gamification technologies

Gamification emerged as a significant trend during this decade, especially in the field of e-learning. While the concept of gamification was introduced in 2002, it gained popularity in the education sector during this decade. Gamification refers to the use of game design elements in non-game contexts, such as education, medicine, team building, etc. The use of gamification in e-learning made the learning experience more engaging, interactive, and fun for students. Gamification elements, such as points, badges, and leaderboards, provided learners with instant feedback and the motivation to complete their learning tasks.

Mobile learning and mobile apps

One of the most significant developments during this time was the widespread adoption of mobile devices, which led to the development of mobile learning or m-learning. M-learning allowed learners to access course materials and participate in online courses using their smartphones and tablets, making learning more flexible and accessible. Subsequently, mobile apps (experiences designed specifically for mobile phones) emerged as another significant development during this decade. Educational apps, such as Duolingo, Khan Academy, were among the front runners, providing learners with a range of learning resources, such as videos, quizzes, and games.

Adaptive learning

Another significant development during this decade was the emergence of the concept of adaptive learning. Adaptive learning technologies use data analytics and machine learning (ML) algorithms to personalize the learning experience for individual learners based on their learning preferences and performance. Personalized learning refers to providing learners with customized learning experiences based on their unique learning preferences, interests, and abilities. Personalized learning can take many forms, such as adaptive learning, competency-based learning, and personalized assessments. One example of an adaptive learning platform is Knewton, which uses data analytics to create personalized learning pathways for learners.

Virtual and augmented reality

Virtual reality (VR) and augmented reality (AR) emerged as significant trends during this decade, providing learners with immersive learning experiences. VR and AR enabled learners to explore and interact with complex concepts in a three-dimensional environment. For example, medical students could use VR to simulate surgeries, which provided them with a realistic learning experience. Although VR has been around for several decades, it became more accessible and affordable only during the last decade, thanks to technological advancements.

1/ DIGITAL REVOLUTION IN LEARNING TECHNOLOGIES

2019-2023: Digital explosions

The COVID-19 pandemic has significantly impacted students' education, with many schools, colleges, and universities being forced to function virtually with the use of artificial intelligence (AI) tools. Thus, the third decade of the 21st century has seen a significant increase in the use of AI and personalized learning. AI has the potential to transform the way education is delivered and consumed, making it more personalized, adaptive, and efficient.

Remote and virtual learning

Remote and virtual learning has led to an explosion in e-learning, as educators and learners have had to adapt to new ways of teaching and learning because of the pandemic. The pandemic highlighted the need for flexible, adaptive, and resilient learning systems that could withstand disruptions in direct learning due to unforeseen events. An example of the e-learning explosion during the pandemic is the use of video conferencing tools, such as Zoom and Microsoft Teams. These tools were widely adopted for remote teaching and learning. It allowed teachers and learners to connect in real time, even when they were physically distant from each other.

According to Statista[1], 70% of organizations in 2020 suggested that they are investing in virtual learning delivery systems. However, the definition includes the latest virtual means such as AR, VR, and metaverse.

Hybrid learning

With the success of remote learning during the COVID-19 pandemic, followed by eased cross-border restrictions among some countries,

---

[1] 10 eLearning Software Trends for 2022/2023. https://financesonline.com/elearning-software-trends/

hybrid learning emerged as a powerful learning mechanism that allowed both onsite and remote learners to leverage a mixture of technologies. Boston.com's 2020 surveys suggested that 80% of the students chose the hybrid learning model over traditional ones. Most organizations replaced instructor-led events with remote or virtual training sessions by leveraging their previously mastered blended learning models. This allowed the flexibility of having virtual learning and the intensity of in-person learning into one. However, several technological challenges are associated with the process, making it difficult for the facilitators to have this model in place.

Microlearning

Another significant development during this decade was the increased focus on microlearning. Microlearning involves breaking down learning content into small, bite-sized modules that can be accessed and completed quickly. This approach to learning is particularly beneficial to busy professionals, who usually have limited time for learning. The e-learning industry reported in 2021 that around 94% of L&D professionals prefer microlearning to other e-learning tools.

Online proctoring

Online proctoring is another significant development that has emerged in recent years. It refers to the use of technology to monitor and verify students' identity and activity during exams or assessments. With the shift of educational institutions to online learning, online proctoring has become increasingly popular since it provides a means to ensure academic integrity in remote environments.

1/ DIGITAL REVOLUTION IN LEARNING TECHNOLOGIES

Immersive VR/AR technologies

Another emerging trend in the e-learning industry is the use of highly immersive, multisensory VR and AR to create immersive learning experiences. VR and AR can simulate real-world environments and provide learners with hands-on, interactive learning experiences. Both technologies are particularly well suited to training and education in fields such as healthcare and engineering. Microsoft Corporation has developed HoloLens, an AR headset that can be used to simulate real-world scenarios in fields such as healthcare and engineering. VR and AR technologies have become more accessible and affordable, making them increasingly popular in digital learning.

Natural language processing (NLP) AI

The concept of AI has been around for several decades now; however, it has gained more attention in education only during this decade. AI refers to the use of technology to perform tasks that normally require human intelligence, such as problem-solving, decision-making, and natural language processing (NLP). AI has the potential to transform education in several ways, such as providing personalized learning experiences, automating administrative tasks, and improving student outcomes. AI-powered tools, such as chatbots and intelligent tutoring systems, are already used in education to provide learners with instant feedback, answers to questions, and personalized support. AI is a trend that has the potential to revolutionize digital learning.

Blockchain technology

Blockchain technology has also emerged as a potential solution to some of the challenges the education sector faces, such as credentialing, verification, and data security. The technology is a decentralized digital ledger that records transactions across multiple computers, making them resistant to tampering or modification. In the education sector, blockchain technology can be used to verify academic credentials, securely store student records, and ensure data privacy and security.

2023-2030: Emergence of parallel worlds

While COVID-19 accelerated the adoption of a range of technologies, the early signs and revolutionary developments during the post-COVID period (2022–2023) show signs that the landscape of learning and HR technologies are no longer going to be the same as those during the beginning of the decade. As we look ahead to the remaining years of this decade, I am sure that several newer trends and technologies will likely shape the spectrum of learning technologies.

Increased use of AI and ML

One of the most significant forecasts for the eLearning industry in the next decade is the increased use of AI and ML. These technologies can be used to personalize the learning experience, provide real-time feedback, and automate certain aspects of the learning process. AI and ML can help identify the individual learning preferences of the participants/students and tailor the educational modules accordingly to meet their learning needs. These technologies can also be used to automate tasks such as grading and assessment, freeing up educators' time and enabling them to focus on more complex tasks.

1/ DIGITAL REVOLUTION IN LEARNING TECHNOLOGIES

Increased adoption of VR/AR

One significant forecast for the eLearning industry in the next decade is the increased adoption of VR/AR technologies. VR/AR can be used to create immersive learning experiences that simulate real-world scenarios and provide hands-on, interactive learning opportunities. For example, VR/AR can be used in medical education to simulate surgical procedures or in engineering education to provide virtual simulations of equipment and machinery. This technology can also be used to create interactive virtual classrooms where learners can collaborate and interact with each other in a virtual environment.

Metaverse immersive environment

While metaverse (an immersive environment by Facebook) is in its nascent phases, gamified virtual immersive technologies are already being used in complex job roles that require a range of technologies, from computing to vision processing to sensor technologies, in order to make learning multisensory. Such development crosses the boundaries of traditional computer or software-driven technologies and brings learning into a human-machine realm. Continuous shift of microlearning into nanolearning

As the current generation's attention span is becoming shorter as a result of the world becoming fast-paced, microlearning is shifting toward learning through bite-sized modules, called nanolearning, that can be absorbed on the go via mobiles. This approach to learning is particularly well-suited to the needs of busy professionals who may have limited time for learning. Nanolearning helps improve learners' retention and engagement as well as makes learning more accessible and flexible. It can be delivered through a range of platforms and devices, including smartphones and tablets, and can be used to provide just-in-time (JIT) learning opportunities as well.

STRATEGIC LEARNING TECHNOLOGY LEADERSHIP

Increased focus on soft skills

In addition to technical skills, there is likely to be an increased focus on soft skills, such as communication, collaboration, and problem-solving, in the next decade. These skills are becoming increasingly important in the modern workplace, where teamwork and adaptability are essential. E-learning can be an effective way to develop these skills through collaborative learning activities and simulations. For example, virtual team projects can allow learners to develop communication and collaboration skills in a safe and supportive environment.

Greater integration of social media

Social media is likely to become increasingly integrated into e-learning platforms and tools in the next decade. According to Thinkific's *Digital Learning Trends 2023 report*[a], the world is expected to see a rise in community-first digital learning. While digital communities or forums have traditionally been an add-on to existing courses or learning products, it is undeniable that they will soon move toward as the main play to building e-learning.

Social media can be used to support collaborative learning and provide opportunities for learners to connect and engage with each other. For example, social media facilitates peer feedback and discussion, providing learners access to a broader network of professionals and experts. Social media can also be used to provide personalized learning recommendations based on learners' interests and activities.

As we look ahead to the next decade, it is clear that learning technologies will continue to play a significant role in education and

---

[a]https://www.thinkific.com/elearning-trends/

training. We can expect to see further advancements in learning technologies driven by the heightened needs of learners who want more immersive experiences.

TAKING IT FORWARD

Through a brief account of the emergence of the digital revolution, this chapter puts forth a viewpoint that implementing learning technologies in complex environments is far more strategic and complex than it was years ago. Thus, there is a need for strategic leaders in specialized roles to lead the learning technologies domain in order to stay ahead in organizational competitiveness.

Use the space below to reflect upon and note down your major takeaways from this chapter.

Reflections 1.1

Chapter 1
DIGITAL REVOLUTION IN LEARNING TECHNOLOGIES

Chapter 2
BUSINESS KPIs FOR LEARNING TECHNOLOGY

Chapter 3
STRATEGIC LEARNING TECHNOLOGY LEADERSHIP THINKING

Chapter 4
TECHNOLOGIES & ANALYTICS FOR HIRING RIGHT

Chapter 5
TECHNOLOGIES & ANALYTICS FOR PROFICIENCY METRICS

Chapter 6
TECHNOLOGIES & ANALYTICS FOR WORK SKILLS

Chapter 7
TECHNOLOGIES & ANALYTICS FOR EFFICIENT LEARNING PATH

Chapter 8
TECHNOLOGIES & ANALYTICS FOR TIME MEASUREMENTS

Chapter 9
EMERGING TECHNOLOGIES FOR SPEED

Chapter 10
THE FINAL THOUGHTS

BONUS
MODELLING GEN-AI FOR ENTERPRSE L&D

L&D CAREER RESOURCES

2
BUSINESS KPIs FOR LEARNING TECHNOLOGIES

2/ BUSINESS KPIs FOR LEARNING TECHNOLOGIES

The end goal of any learning technology should be to improve knowledge retention, enhance employee engagement, and increase skill development. Such a goal has multiple aspects. With the advent of technologies such as AI, ML, and adaptive learning, the scope of learning technologies is becoming more complex, diverse, and cross-functional. There is a complex mesh of options across software, platforms, applications/apps, and solutions that need to be evaluated in order to deliver highly efficient and cost-effective learning. Increased globalization, borderless working, and increased remote working have resulted in scalability challenges. Most of the technologies continue to be cloud-hosted, sharing infrastructure with other competing organizations while also being concerned about data security and safety. At the same time, most technologies are becoming expensive and capital-intensive due to the sheer size and scale of implementation. Thus, the learning technologies space is no longer straightforward. Such a complex function requires far more strategic viewpoint and well-established key performance indicators (KPIs) to govern successful implementation.

BUSINESS LANDSCAPE

Businesses use learning technologies depending on the scale of operations. Not all businesses rely on learning technologies. However, during the recent pandemic, we saw several mid-scale organizations thriving profitably and making revenues at a surprisingly high rate that was never possible before. But, at the same time, we saw thousands of large vintage businesses collapse. As I analyzed the scenario, I realized that the one thing differentiating the successful businesses from those that shut down was their ability to quickly leverage a range of learning technologies flexibly to continue enabling employees in the field even during the lockdown.

On top of that, the pandemic fueled technological innovation at a rate never seen before. This emerged as another factor that helped in the survival of organizations that deployed technologies faster than the pace of business, beating their competitors. The key point to note is how these organizations strategically deployed and leveraged technology to increase the speed of employee development, which, in turn, accelerated innovative solutions into the market.

The technology-driven and technology-backed success of organizations that thrived during the pandemic is largely attributed to learning technologies. However, the real heroes behind business continuity during the time of the pandemic were those learning technologists who were highly strategic in their leadership and could successfully architect company-wide solutions at a rapid pace. In the current era, selection, testing, implementation, obsolescence, and upgrading of workplace and learning technologies require higher-order strategic thinking where the person could rub shoulders with C-suite executives to push their innovations.

We see a positive change whereby forward-thinking organizations have begun recognizing learning technologies as the core strategic function of their organizational learning endeavors.

Historically, organizations have relied heavily on general IT or functional IT folks with broader experience in infrastructure implementation to push the technological needs of various business units. That kind of approach might work well for most business units and operations. Ironically, their emphasis used to be limited to 'things' (like technologies). They continued to miss the point that technologies need to be managed, keeping humans in mind in terms of how human development, learning, skills, and performance could be accelerated using technologies.

Any learning and training business is run differently. Without knowing how learning processes work and which technologies are effective, one cannot decide to implement the correct solutions to speed up employee learning and development. As technologies are becoming both complex and interdependent, most of the learning technologies are diverging into a range of capabilities across functions. They need strategic learning technology leadership to identify the gaps, process requirements, and technological requirements to develop strategies for integrating them into the organization's learning initiatives. Thus, organizations need dedicated learning technology leaders with highest order strategic thinking.

With the advent of new technologies such as VR, AI, and ML, the way we learn is changing rapidly. Organizations need to stay on top of these trends and ensure that their learning initiatives are up-to-date and effective. With the accelerating technological changes, we observe several organizations struggling to keep up with the skills needed to compete in the digital age. By developing strategic learning technology leadership, an organization can ensure that an organization's learning technology strategies are truly strategic and built for speed. In turn, this allows other functions to institute initiatives that are effective, efficient, and aligned with its overall strategic objectives.

Big data and analytics enable organizations to track and analyze learner behavior and gain insights into what works and what doesn't. Learning analytics can provide valuable insights into the effectiveness of learning initiatives as well as areas for improvement. However, a strategic viewpoint is needed to understand the capabilities of analytics platforms and develop strategies for technology that can optimize their learning initiatives and improve learning outcomes. This will allow employees to acquire new skills and knowledge throughout their careers, improving employee retention and supporting the organization's long-term goals and objectives. Such strategic leadership ensures that the organization gets the maximum value in return for its investment in technology.

If organizations wish to taste strategic success and want to stay competitive in this fast-paced world, they need learning technology strategic leadership.

THE TECHNOLOGY ROI TRAP

If you are a learning technology leader, your biggest challenge would be presenting, defending, and measuring the ROI of capital-intensive learning technologies. Your executives always want you to compute and present the ROI of the technology pre-implementation and would insist on proving that planned ROI is indeed achieved post-implementation. Thus, no matter what, you still need to make defendable proposals to introduce new technologies.

However, as you are aware, most of the learning and HR tech folks fail to demonstrate good ROI. The best that they demonstrate is a fabricated or 'imagined' ROI. This is because they do not use relevant metrics to compute the ROI values. Without clear metrics to demonstrate the value of learning-related technologies, building buy-in and support for future learning and technology projects can be challenging.

2/ BUSINESS KPIs FOR LEARNING TECHNOLOGIES

Unreal metrics for learning technology ROI

Why would you want to implement powerful technologies in your organization? Whenever I ask this question to learning technology leaders, most of them mention reasons related to the efficiency, effectiveness, automation, cost-effectiveness, and scalability of their learning programs. This might sound counterintuitive, but most learning technologists are so passionate about learning technologies to the point that they often bring new technological solutions for the sake of looking cool. Sadly, they start technology implementation on the wrong foot. In fact, I found in my research that poorly implemented learning technologies are the biggest cause of not only inefficiency but also the slowdown of employee development. However, most learning technology professionals will not admit it. They try to find a shortcut by using metrics such as training durations and associated costs to prove that they are doing a great job.

I noticed that many of them also cite 'efficiency,' that is, 'doing things faster' or similar connotations of productivity as one of the pressing arguments for technology implementation. However, my research in the book *Accelerated Proficiency in Accelerated Times* questions that connotation. Asking employees to do tasks faster, deliver faster, or finish projects faster is not something that could give your organization a competitive edge. The real speed that matters is how fast your employees are developed to the desired proficiency, where they can produce products that are far more revolutionary and also faster than your competitors.

But, most technology leaders refrain from powerful metrics that require measuring, tracking, and reporting the speed of employee development. They avoid such metrics because they metrics are either hard to measure or do not paint a rosy picture of technology effectiveness. So, their best fallback is to use surveys or qualitative 'feel' of users. This over-reliance or over-emphasis on pure training scalability-related or learning effectiveness-related metrics does nothing more than end up with technology that is a white elephant on corporate infrastructure.

The real metrics for learning technology ROI

First, let us recalibrate. Think for a moment. As a learning technology leader, why would you exist in an organization? What is that single thing you will be required to deliver?

The answer might be shocking to you! It is not the technology implementation....It is the speed of employee development! Your single most important, and perhaps the only, KPI that should matter is how fast employees are developing by implementing or leveraging a specific learning technology. If your employees are not learning fast enough, not developing fast enough, not attaining the desired proficiency at a faster rate, and not able to gain experience fast enough to deliver their outcomes, then there is no point in having the world's most innovative learning technologies in your organization. If you cannot deliver the expected speed of employee development at the speed of business, your role is questionable.

The workforce needs to acquire next-generation skills and master never-seen-before technologies or products. Today, technology is the first line of defense that impacts how employees learn, develop, and perform in the workplace. However, not all managers and leaders are fully educated about setting up a holistic ecosystem and technological infrastructure focused on increasing the speed of employee development.

2/ BUSINESS KPIs FOR LEARNING TECHNOLOGIES

Let us analyze this now…Imagine that somehow you are able to demonstrate that your implementation of the new technology can cut one month of learning or development time for one employee. In that case, you can right away translate it to dollar savings for over 2000 employees and then compound it to over 5 years. However, most learning technology leaders are not taught this revolutionary approach. Once you learn this, you will find that even your CEO cannot refute the impact when presented with this perspective of cutting the time from the development journey.

The key is to use the speed of employee development as your KPI and ultimate deliverable. Based on my experience, I can tell you that this is the single most 'make-or-break' challenge. You can master it by identifying the correct data and analytics to measure the effectiveness of learning technologies or any infrastructure-related initiatives. Without these data, making informed decisions and even justifying the ROI of learning technology can be challenging.

In the following sections, you will learn time-to-proficiency (TTP) as the metrics associated with the speed of employee learning and development and the rate of performance improvement and how these metrics guide the technology selection, implementation, and justification of an irrefutable ROI of learning technologies. Mastering the science of this KPI will guide you in the transformation of learning technology infrastructure. Let us learn 'how to represent and measure the speed of employee development.'

MEASURING EMPLOYEE DEVELOPMENT

When an employee takes up a new role or job, we provide orientation or onboarding interventions, formal training, or coaching; we then provide them with on-the-job support and tools. We provide the employees with everything that is required to accelerate their career path, as shown in Figure 2.1. What is the end goal of that path?

Meaning of proficiency

We aim to make our employees fully proficient in their jobs as soon as possible. So, what does proficiency mean?

Every job has some performance measures or KPIs. We want employees to deliver those KPIs as soon as possible. For instance, let us assume that a salesperson's performance measure is sales worth 1 million dollars per month; here, proficiency refers to generating a minimum of that much every month. However, just being a one-time hit wonder is not proficiency. We need to measure his/her performance over a period of time, say 3 or 6 months. That steady state is called proficiency or proficient performance. Thus, proficiency is a state of performance at which performers consistently produce business outcomes or deliverables to the set performance thresholds of a given job role. It refers to achieving and maintaining one pre-established performance level and does not imply progression through different stages or levels of performance. It refers to the business performance of the job role and does not convey an individual's performance demonstrated in a single task or skill.

At this proficient performance stage, your teams deliver at least the agreed threshold defined for their job roles. They provide a repeatable performance—you can be sure of it. Their outcomes are reliable—you can depend upon them. They deliver consistently. They are independently productive, and they do not need much supervision.

2/ BUSINESS KPIs FOR LEARNING TECHNOLOGIES

Figure 2.1: Employee development journey.

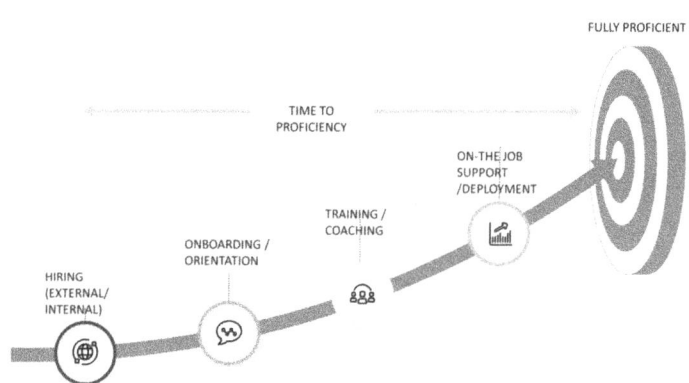

TTP metrics

Let me use a visual graph to make a point. Figure 2.2 is a hypothetical proficiency–time chart. It is a simplistic representation of an employee's proficiency growth over time.

The dotted horizontal line is the target proficiency that you want your employees to reach. For instance, it could be $1 million in sales.

If you do not put in deliberate efforts, the employees will start working in their own way following the 'normal proficiency curve.' They will reach the target proficiency in a certain time. We call it time-to-proficiency (TTP). It is usually measured from the start of a job role or the date of hiring to reach the point of being independently productive. With no interventions from your side, employees might reach the desired proficiency level in time T1.

Figure 2.2: Proficiency–time graph.

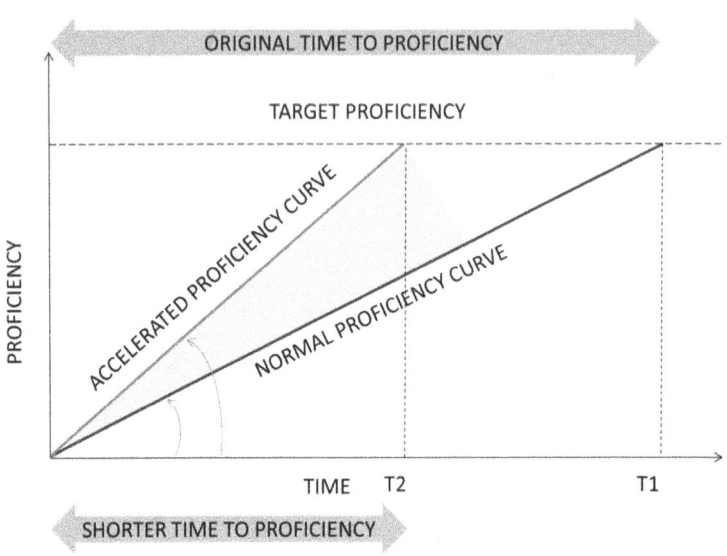

You have recently experienced during the pandemic that you could not wait for employees to take a natural path. You needed them to master new technologies, new working methods, and new skills in almost no time.

Perhaps that was the first time you wondered if there were ways to lift up that slope of the proficiency curve in a way that employees could follow an 'accelerated proficiency curve,' as shown in Figure 2.2. The employees are likely to attain the same desired proficiency in a shorter time, T2.

An employee's TTP metrics in a job tell us how slow or fast he/she is going compared to the market baseline. Employees, irrespective of their job role, require a certain amount of time to reach the level of proficiency desired by the organization they are associated with. The whole idea of speeding up employee performance is to measure and shorten TTP metrics.

A few clarifications about TTP are needed at this point.

- TTP does not apply only to newly hired employees. It applies equally to employees transferred from one job role to another.
- TTP does not always mean the onboarding time.
- TTP is not measured based on just a single activity; rather, it involves the collective time required for several activities such as onboarding, formal training, informal training, on-the-job training, projects, and other activities to gain experience on specific tasks or skills required to do the work.
- TTP is not measured at one employee level but at the entire job role level and is usually averaged across all employees serving that job role.
- TTP is not equal to the time taken to get trained on basic skills to start the job.
- TTP indicates the real time taken to produce the job outcomes consistently and independently.

Distinction among similar terms

There are other equivalent terms used to denote TTP. But, they have some notable differences. *Time to complete training* is wrongly called *time-to-proficiency*, but it is not. It simply conveys the time it takes for an individual to finish a training program. A shorter time to complete training indicates that the employee has been taught the necessary skills in a shorter time, but it does not convey if he/she has attained the target proficiency. Literature uses terms like *time-to-first success*, which measures the time from the beginning of a training program to the first instance of success, such as the completion of a task or project without assistance. It is an indication of the effectiveness of training programs and also the employees' time to competence. *Time to competence* measures the time it takes for an individual to demonstrate competence in his/her role, as measured against predefined performance standards or benchmarks. Typically, delivering performance or competence once is not an indication of proficiency, and it has to be repeatable, reliable, and consistent for a fairly long period of time.

Organizations often use the *time to full productivity* term, which measures the time it takes for an employee to reach his/her full potential in his/her role, contributing toward the highest possible level of productivity. In most cases, it denotes proficiency if productivity is a measure used to define proficiency in the first place.

Another similar term is *time to mastery*, which measures the time it takes for an individual to achieve a level of expertise or mastery in his/her role, which is typically demonstrated by consistently high performance. Normally, mastery and expertise convey elite status far beyond standard proficiency, which is typically expected from employees. In a large population of employees, there are only a handful of experts or masters.

KNOWING TTP METRICS

We need to understand why TTP metrics are so important in an organizational context. There are two aspects: First, the magnitude of TTP durations makes it worrisome for leaders. Second, the

2/ BUSINESS KPIs FOR LEARNING TECHNOLOGIES

business drivers force leaders to think about the importance of these metrics.

TTP is usually so long that it has an adverse effect on employee competitiveness. I conducted a research study across 66 project cases across several job functions. As seen in Table 2.1, the magnitude of TTP was seen to be an upside of 3 years. For instance, TTP in technical jobs spanned 2 months to several years, depending on the industry. In scientific or R&D jobs, people took anywhere between 6 months to 3 years to become proficient.

Also note that TTP was several times higher when compared with the time to train the employees. As a matter of fact, the function of training is no more than providing basic skills to get started. No amount of training can ensure building proficiency to the desired level. Employees need to get engaged in several experience-building activities to become consistent in their performance.

Table 2.1: Magnitude of TTP across different primary job types

Primary job nature	Count of cases	Time to training	TTP
Technical or engineering	16	5 to 18 weeks	2 months to several years
Sales—non-technical	5	1 to 10 weeks	3 months to 1.5 years
Scientific or development	4	No data	6 months to 3 years
Customer service helpdesk	4	4 to 12 weeks	1.5 months to 1 year
Sales—technical	3	No data	Unknown to 1.5 years
Managerial, supervisory	3	4 to 13 weeks	1 month to 14 months

Strategic management, leadership	3	No data	1 year to very long#
Medical, healthcare	3		3 months to 1 year
Production, manufacturing	3		1 month to 5 months*
Financial services	2	15 weeks	5 months to 3 years
Training or education	1	No data	1 to 2 years
Assembly, repair	1		1 week

#Exceptions: Some rare events that happen once in 10-20 years (e.g., managers having to handle declining gold prices).

*Exceptions: Some rare events that happen once in 8–10 years events (e.g., miners dealing with underground fires).

MARKET PRESSURES FOR SPEED

There is a consensus that the time to achieve a higher level of proficiency to do any job consistently and reliably with a high degree of repeatability is generally very long. The fact is that organizations do not have that time! Market pressure, particularly in the last decade, has warranted accelerating the expertise cycle as a necessity. Unpredicted disasters like the COVID-19 pandemic have opened the eyes of most L&D leaders. They now associate market competitiveness as a function of how fast the workforce can learn new skills to face future challenges. They have realized that the traditional approach of preparing employees for predictable situations is no longer a recipe for a competitive edge. The future is ambiguous and unpredictable! So, it is the need of the hour for employees to master the skills quickly to the desired level in a much shorter time in order to be able to handle unpredictable challenges.

2/ BUSINESS KPIs FOR LEARNING TECHNOLOGIES

When an employee takes longer to become proficient, it has repercussions on the business. Several market forces collectively drive the need for a shorter TTP in the workplace, such as time-to-market competitiveness; constant obsolescence of skills; the increasing complexity of jobs and skills; and attrition of senior or aging workforce constantly getting replaced.

The magnitude and scale show us its impact on the business. The larger the magnitude and scale of the TTP, the more significant the business impact. Thus, the larger the push for organizations to think about shortening TTP.

In my research, I categorized these forces into four business drivers: time-related pressures, speed-related competitiveness, skill-related deficiencies, and cost/financial implications. These four drivers are summarized in Table 2.2 in terms of the nature of factors that push organizations to do something about the long TTP of employees.

Table 2.2: Definition of business drivers

Drivers	Definition	Examples
Time-related pressures	The drivers in which operational metrics were consciously measured in the unit of time.	The time required to launch a product, The actual length of TTP longer training duration
Speed-related competitiveness	The operational metrics in which speed was perceived as a measure of success.	Customer pressures to deliver fast; market urgencies to produce fast; business ramp-up speed;

		The speed of launch of a new product, service, or business;
		The need for rapid operational readiness;
		Rapid hiring sprints
Skill-related deficiencies	The needs arise because of a lack of workforce skills or a lack of a qualified workforce.	Attrition and retirement;
		New hires replacing expert workforce;
		Performance issues due to a lack of skills and obsolete skills
Cost or financial implications	The factors and impacts were measured in the unit of money.	The cost of training, the cost of someone not being proficient;
		Errors and mistakes;
		The cost of opportunity lost while someone was not proficient;
		Regulatory pressures that cost the company severely if not observed, such as safety

Time- and speed-related drivers

Time- and speed-related drivers relate to market urgencies such as time-to-market pressures, competitiveness, and business pressures, among other factors. With the pace of technology, time-to-market pressure on the workforce is increasing to acquire complex skills at a faster pace. Naturally, organizations that can develop employees at a faster rate would stand out in the competition.

As an organization, you need your employees to design products, solutions, and technologies at the rate of customers' demand. If somehow you could accelerate their learning, they could innovate faster by coming up to speed with newer technologies. In turn, it would allow you to shorten the time-to-market of your products or services and meet customer expectations at a faster rate. That's the key to staying ahead of the competition.

Skill deficiency-related drivers

Third drivers relate to skill-deficiency-related business drivers, which include challenges like the retiring workforce, the complexity of jobs, and the changing nature of work. These are the most foundational drivers. That means, even if everything has a dollar value, the capabilities and speed with which you develop employees are the most fundamental drivers to consider while attempting to shorten TTP. Once you close the skills gaps faster or prepare the workforce at a higher speed, the chain reaction is a better time and speed advantage, better time-to-market performance, and better cost-efficiency.

You have to see skill deficiency in the context of the environment. According to a study by Deloitte (2017), the half-life of any skill in 2017 was shrinking to 1.5 years. Today, we expect it to be even shorter. That means any skill you acquire today would be obsolete within 2-3 years. You and your learners have no choice but to learn and master new skills much faster to stay relevant and productive. The shelf life of skills during the pandemic is seen roughly as roughly 3 to 6 months, which will squeeze down further in the post-COVID era. The time-to-market of new products and services is close to 3 months.

But more concerning is the time to master new skills or solutions, which is a rough upside of one year. It is a catch-22. It leads to two challenges. The first is how to hire fast, and the second is how to develop them quickly after hiring. Thus, there is a strong business case for speeding up learning at the workplace.

However, several non-financial reasons, such as the impact of non-proficiency in critical professions, are also equally important. For example, in a study involving firefighting commanders, the lack of events to gain experience and become proficient was perceived to endanger life and property when those events occurred, requiring proficient people to handle them. Therefore, the business has a pressing need to accelerate the speed-to-proficiency of their employees in almost every job.

Cost-related drivers

Several studies indicated substantial financial or cost benefits of shorter training duration and faster workforce readiness from the reduction of TTP. Imagine an employee working for you takes one year to become good at his job. That's a massive amount of cost and opportunity lost. This is a foundational reason why we would need accelerated workplace learning. If you prepare learners or employees at a faster rate, they will make fewer mistakes. It means a considerable sum of money is saved that otherwise would be incurred to address those mistakes. This also means saving on account of costly retraining.

The skill-deficiency-related business drivers are the most foundational. That means, even if everything has a dollar value, the capabilities and speed with which you develop your employees are the most fundamental drivers to think about while attempting to shorten TTP. Once you close the skill gaps faster or prepare the workforce at a higher speed, the chain reaction is a better time and speed advantage, better time-to-market performance, and better cost-efficiency.

BENEFITS OF SHORTENING TTP

In my book titled *Speed Matters*, I have explained how speed has become essential in ensuring that employees learn new skills faster and become proficient in delivering business outcomes.

Fred Charles, the father of the term *speed-to-proficiency*, makes a compelling argument in his book Breakaway (2002, p. 16): 'Speed to proficiency is more than a theoretical advantage. It is the most devastating competitive weapon in the world where the competitive forces of scale, automation, and capital are subordinate to the power of proficient workforce.' The efforts to accelerate TTP, thus lead to the faster readiness of the workforce, cost savings, and increased competitiveness in the market.

Irrespective of the actual length, our acceptance of the fact that it takes a long time to achieve proficiency is the basis of accelerating the same. It must be recognized that the TTP business problem is too big for organizations to ignore, and, therefore, organizations must address this business challenge because of the impact it has on the workforce, business metrics, profitability, and market competitiveness.

Sometimes, leaders would associate the length of training or overall TTP directly with the potential cost-saving or the financial gains they can get by reducing it. While this is an undebatable relationship, I observed that the projects that start with the goal of saving costs for employee development might not result in overall better competitiveness. However, cost savings and financial gains are invariably achieved when projects are initiated to gain competitive advantages or skill efficiencies.

Leading workplace learning expert Jay Cross once stated, 'the faster a worker becomes proficient, the more profitable the firm.' Similarly, in their book *Learning Paths*, leading business consultants Rosenbaum & Williams stressed the importance of identifying the point at which desired performance is delivered: 'You need to know the level of performance required to do the job and how long it takes to get there.... when you can get employees up-to speed in far less time, productivity rises at far less expense.'

The faster employees learn the skills required to do the job up to the set performance standards, the faster they will be able to handle new customer needs, meet new market needs, perform to new expectations, and deliver new technologies or adopt new changes. The essence is...Every business leader needs to consider how to shorten that TTP! When you shorten that time, you gain benefits, as shown by the gray area in Figure 2.2, representing dollars saved, improved productivity, and other business benefits. In my research study, I found four types of business benefits of shorter TTP, which are shown in Table 2.3.

Table 2.3: Nature of business benefits of shorter TTP

Benefits	Benefits as seen by 50 organizations
Business gains	Increased market share
	Shorter sales cycle
	Increased profit or revenue
	Competitiveness
	Readiness of staff
	Improved sales
	Higher customer satisfaction

2/ BUSINESS KPIs FOR LEARNING TECHNOLOGIES

Improvement in operational metrics	Increase in staff retention
	Need for fewer staff
	More training intakes or capacity
	Shorter courses
	Improvement in skill scores
Improvement in productivity	Improvement in processing rate
	Reduction in errors
	Improved output
	Availability of staff
	Efficiency and saving of time
Cost savings	Shorter TTP
	Shorter training duration
	Less travel is required
	Cost savings aggregated on a larger population

In this era of speed, TTP is becoming one of the most important business metrics for fast-paced technological organizations. Accordingly, organizations worldwide are striving to figure out interventions, systems, and strategies to shorten the TTP of their employees.

The big question is how such benefits can be drawn. The answer is simple: it depends on how you as a learning technology strategist, institute TTP metrics as a system rather than as another measurement tool. In the following chapter, you will learn about the components of such a strategic framework.

TAKING IT FORWARD

In this chapter, you learned why the speed of employee development is the most devastating competitive weapon in the fast-paced world. In the era of technological and digital revolution, at the onset of Industry 4.0, technology is naturally viewed as the first line of defense for organizations to accelerate employee learning, development, and performance. You realized that, as a strategic learning technology leader, you need to take a strategic stance, which involves implementing technologies to shorten the TTP of the workforce. In the following chapter, you will learn the ingredients of strategic leadership for learning technology implementation.

Use the space below to reflect upon and note down your major takeaways to this point.

2/ BUSINESS KPIs FOR LEARNING TECHNOLOGIES

Reflections 3.1

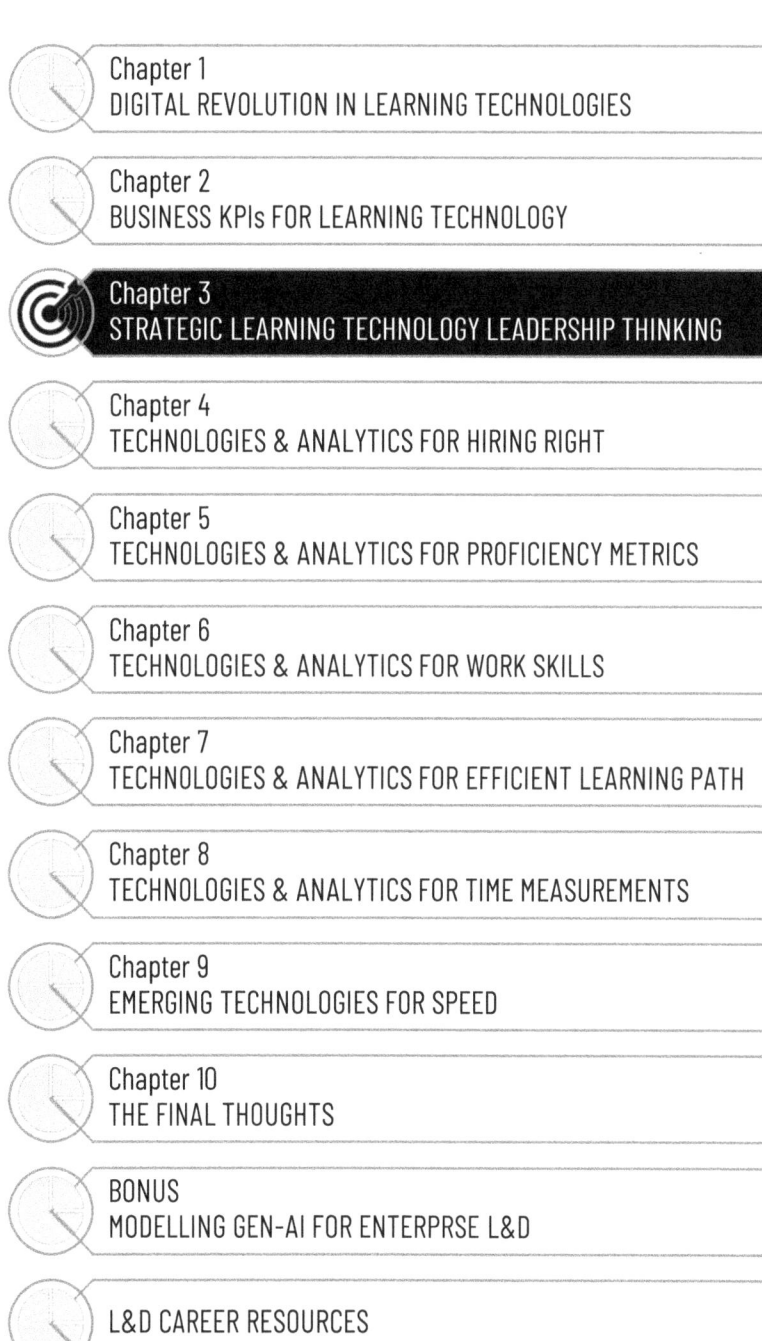

Chapter 1
DIGITAL REVOLUTION IN LEARNING TECHNOLOGIES

Chapter 2
BUSINESS KPIs FOR LEARNING TECHNOLOGY

**Chapter 3
STRATEGIC LEARNING TECHNOLOGY LEADERSHIP THINKING**

Chapter 4
TECHNOLOGIES & ANALYTICS FOR HIRING RIGHT

Chapter 5
TECHNOLOGIES & ANALYTICS FOR PROFICIENCY METRICS

Chapter 6
TECHNOLOGIES & ANALYTICS FOR WORK SKILLS

Chapter 7
TECHNOLOGIES & ANALYTICS FOR EFFICIENT LEARNING PATH

Chapter 8
TECHNOLOGIES & ANALYTICS FOR TIME MEASUREMENTS

Chapter 9
EMERGING TECHNOLOGIES FOR SPEED

Chapter 10
THE FINAL THOUGHTS

BONUS
MODELLING GEN-AI FOR ENTERPRSE L&D

L&D CAREER RESOURCES

3

STRATEGIC LEARNING TECHNOLOGY LEADERSHIP THINKING

3/ STRATEGIC LEARNING TECHNOLOGY LEADERSHIP THINKING

As a seasoned learning technologist or HR technology professional, you may have experienced how fast technologies are becoming obsolete. Selecting the appropriate technologies for workplace requirements is a far more complex and challenging endeavor. This chapter highlights what kind of strategic stance to take when instituting learning, HR, and other technologies.

Strategic technology leadership refers to the ability of an organization's leaders to effectively integrate technology into the company's long-term strategies and goals. This type of leadership focuses on leveraging technology collectively at both the departmental and organizational levels to drive innovation, improve operational efficiency, and create a competitive advantage in the market.

Strategic technology leadership is essential for organizations to maintain a competitive edge in the market; adapt to rapidly changing technology landscapes; drive innovation and growth; optimize operational efficiency; and ensure long-term success and sustainability.

KEEPING HUMANS AT THE CENTER

As mentioned earlier, the key is that technology implementation projects should place humans at the center of their development programs. Employee development and training should aim to invest in personnel to improve their knowledge and skills, and enhance their potential for career growth. Technology can play a crucial role in this process, providing innovative solutions that can support employee learning and development.

However, the best learning experiences involve a combination of technological solutions and human support, such as mentoring, coaching, and feedback. Thus, it is crucial to remember that technology should not replace human interaction or personalized learning experiences.

Moreover, many technologies focus primarily on improving work processes rather than developing employees. For example, collaboration tools have become popular in recent years, and studies have shown that they enhance the way employees work together. While these tools can improve team productivity and communication, they do not necessarily increase the speed of employee development.

There is also a danger that technologies can create a 'one-size-fits-all' approach to employee development, which may not meet employees' individual needs and aspirations. A successful development plan should provide opportunities that meet employees' aspirations, helping them feel valued and interested in their work.

As a tech decision-maker in an organization, it is important to be sensitive to the fact that new technologies do not always make workflows more efficient than before. Sometimes, changing things to fit the technology can actually make things less efficient. Therefore, decision-makers should evaluate how a new technology can accelerate the path to proficiency, and not simply do the work fast or get more work done in a shorter time. You could do so by making sure that you keep humans at the center. After all, any technology you introduce is for humans! Ironically, we've become so tech-savvy that we have forgotten humans out of the equation.

Technology needs to give people a sense of achievement, accomplishment, completion, belongingness, connection, and speed. For example, a healthcare organization may introduce VR simulations to train doctors and nurses on complex medical procedures. This technology enhances the learning experience while still providing a human touch through personalized feedback and mentoring from experienced mentors. But, it should not replace human interaction. Decision-makers must prioritize technologies that accelerate the path to proficiency while keeping humans at the center of the process.

FLAWS IN TRADITIONAL TECHNOLOGY DECISIONS

As organizations strive to improve employee performance and productivity, using technology to develop employees has become increasingly popular. However, not all organizations effectively choose and implement technologies that can speed up employee performance and development paths. In my research, I noticed four significant flaws in organizational decision-making during technological implementation. The larger the organization, the higher the intensity of such flawed decisions.

1) Speed measurements such as TTP are not considered key KPIs for HR and/or learning leaders are held accountable for.
2) Most technologies are procured to improve efficiency rather than speed up TTP.
3) Most technologies are selected or decided by big guys who are not end users.
4) Most technologies assume employees as resources rather than dealing with them as humans.

In the following sections, I shall briefly elaborate on these flaws.

1. Operational KPIs first, not speed of employee development

While HR departments have KPIs for tracking and managing various aspects of the workforce, such as education profiles, diversity distributions, retention ratios, and time to hire, they often overlook the importance of measuring the speed of employee development. Speed, in this context, refers to the rate at which employees are able to acquire new skills and adapt to changing business needs.

The sustainable speed metrics are not their KPI because they don't have a good mechanism to know if they are developing employees fast enough compared to the market. This lack of is a significant challenge for HR departments as they are unable to track and improve the speed of employee development over time.

Moreover, the HR function is often at the mercy of the organization. Many organizations lack a culture of speed; at best, they create a false sense of speed by pushing their employees hard to complete the required tasks. This does not contribute to developing employees faster.

For example, consider a retail organization with a high employee turnover rate due to low employee engagement. HR may focus on KPIs such as time to hire and retention ratios. Still, without measuring the speed of employee development, they cannot determine whether the organization is developing employees fast enough to improve their engagement and reduce turnover. By implementing sustainable speed metrics, the HR department can track and improve the speed of employee development over time, which will eventually lead to better employee engagement and reduced turnover.

3/ STRATEGIC LEARNING TECHNOLOGY LEADERSHIP THINKING

Another example is that of a technology company that needs to keep up with rapidly changing technologies. The HR department may focus on KPIs such as education profiles and diversity distributions. Still, without measuring the speed of employee development, they cannot determine whether employees are acquiring new skills and are adapting to the changing business needs fast enough. By implementing sustainable speed metrics, HR can track and improve the speed of employee development over time, which will eventually lead to a more agile and adaptable workforce.

Overall, measuring the speed of employee development is crucial for the HR department of an organization to stay competitive in today's fast-paced business environment. Without sustainable speed metrics, HR would not notice if the workforce is falling behind the competition.

2. Process efficiency, not for speed-enablement

Organizations often procure technologies to improve process efficiency, effectiveness, user experience, and cost savings. While some technologies may be purchased in an effort to look 'cool' in the market or to compete with competitors, the focus of most of technologies continues to be process improvement or efficiency.

The HR department of an organization often looks for technologies or analytics to track people and their work. Such technologies aim to speed up work, make the work more efficient, and eliminate manual work. Even the best organizations tend to put systems and apps in place to measure the time of transaction, such as the time taken to finish an activity, project, or job. However, despite investing millions of dollars and thousands of hours of training, using technologies beyond tracking basic parameters has no impact on the business's bottom line. That is not enough to build faster TTP!

To build faster TTP, organizations need to look for systems, processes, and technologies designed explicitly to increase the speed of employee skill acquisition. They need to be able to measure TTP, not just at the employee level but also at the group, department, and company levels.

Most likely, the technologies are never bought with the goal of speeding up employee development. So, when we talk about speeding up employee development or speed-to-proficiency, a different set of technologies needs to be implemented.

For instance, consider a healthcare organization that needs to train new nurses quickly to meet the rising demand for healthcare services. Instead of relying on traditional HR technologies to track employee data, the organization could invest in technologies that are designed specifically for accelerating nurse training and skill acquisition. These technologies could include simulation training tools, VR environments, and adaptive learning platforms.

Another example is that of a software development company that needs to stay ahead of rapidly changing technologies. The company could invest in technologies that are designed specifically for accelerating software development and improving employee skill acquisition. These technologies could include code-sharing platforms, collaboration tools, and real-time feedback systems.

Thus, to speed up employee development or TTP, organizations need to implement a different set of technologies than the ones they typically procure for process efficiency. By investing in technologies that are designed specifically for accelerating skill acquisition,

3/ STRATEGIC LEARNING TECHNOLOGY LEADERSHIP THINKING

organizations can stay ahead of the competition and build a more agile and adaptable workforce.

3. Procurement decisions by IT team, not the L&D team

In many organizations, the procurement of technologies is not decided by end users but by IT or tech departments. Their KPIs are in terms of successful project implementation, cost savings, or process efficiency. Their KPIs do not focus on speeding up employee development or performance or shortening TTP. This disconnect can lead to the selection of technologies based on criteria such as successful project implementation, cost savings, or process efficiency. What they miss is important criteria like enabling the speeding up of employee development or shortening of TTP. The end result is that technologies so purchases could only make efficient operations but would not enable speedier employee development.

For example, consider a manufacturing company that needs to train new employees quickly to meet production demands. Instead of considering technologies that are designed specifically for accelerating employee skill acquisition, the IT or tech department may focus on technologies that improve supply chain management or streamline production processes.

Another example is that of a financial services company that needs to stay ahead of rapidly changing regulations. Instead of considering technologies that are designed specifically for accelerating employee learning and performance, the IT or tech department may focus on technologies that improve data security or compliance reporting.

Unless we strategically think of technologies in a way that keeps the primary goal of cutting the time out from the employee development journey, no amount of technologies like AI or others will help. Ultimately, to achieve the goal of cutting time out of the employee development journey, organizations need to think strategically about the technologies they procure. They need to consider technologies that are explicitly designed to accelerate employee skill acquisition and performance rather than just focusing on process efficiency or cost savings.

4. Employees are considered things, not humans

In today's context, particularly during and after the pandemic, technologies have played a significant role in speeding up employee proficiency. However, despite the availability of advanced technologies and analytics to track a range of employee data, most organizations tend to see employees as 'resources' (things) rather than humans. This disconnect between data and human contribution can hinder an organization's ability to compete against its competitors.

For example, consider a retail organization that needs to improve its customer service to stay competitive. The organization may track customer service metrics such as wait times and satisfaction ratings. Still, without connecting this data to employee development and performance, they may struggle to improve their customer service speed and quality.

Moreover, HR departments often overlook the importance of integrating analytics and strategies around a common anchor to connect, align, and synthesize incompatible analytics across business

3/ STRATEGIC LEARNING TECHNOLOGY LEADERSHIP THINKING

units. This can hinder an organization's ability to increase the speed of employee development and performance.

To address these challenges, HR departments need to prioritize speed and understand the concept of TTP. In the book *Speed Matters*, I have shared how organizations can use TTP metrics to measure, establish a baseline, and increase the speed of employee performance. For example, a technology company may need to speed up the proficiency of its software developers to stay ahead of rapidly changing technologies. By implementing TTP metrics, the company can track and improve the speed of employee development, leading to a more agile and adaptable workforce.

By integrating analytics and strategies and prioritizing speed and TTP, organizations can improve their ability to compete in today's fast-paced business environment.

STRATEGIC LEARNING TECHNOLOGY LEADERSHIP FRAMEWORK

The strategic technology leadership that I am advocating for here is far beyond the norms of traditional strategic technology leadership inducted in most organizations.

You need to have a broader and more holistic thinking process to function successfully as a strategic learning technology leader. In this chapter, you will learn the three elements of the *Strategic Technology Leadership Framework: Speed-enabling ecosystem, Systems to institute TTP metrics, and Strategic technology thinking*. These have been described below and also shown in Figure 3.1:

Speed-enabling ecosystem within which various technologies work in unison toward shortening TTP.

Systems to institute TTP metrics across departments and integrate the measurement and tracking of such metrics using technologies.

Strategic technology thinking about integrating and synchronizing technologies and analytics anchored to TTP metrics.

Figure 3.1: Strategic learning technology leadership framework.

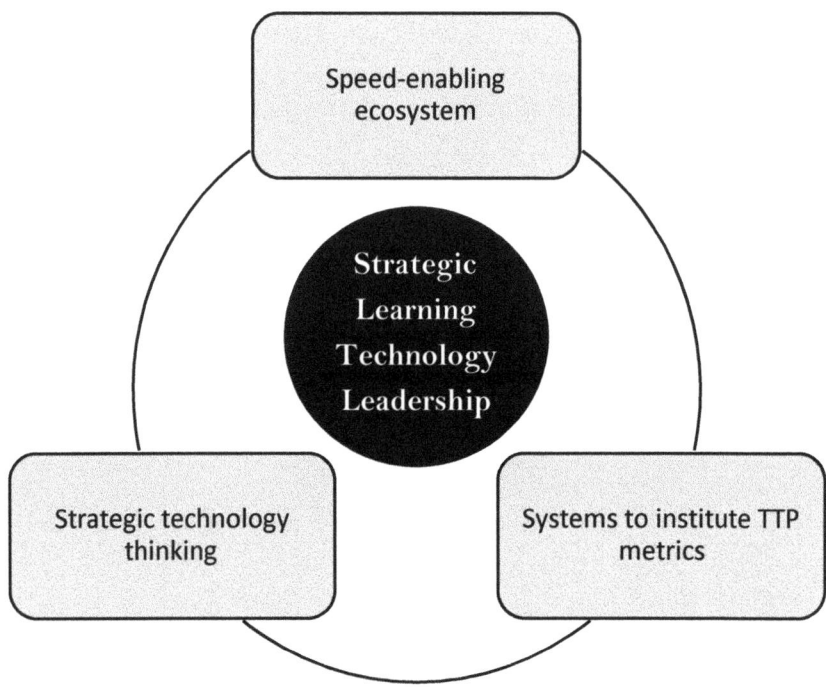

3/ STRATEGIC LEARNING TECHNOLOGY LEADERSHIP THINKING

Speed-enabling technology ecosystem

When strategizing technologies for speed of employee development, you need to consider the architecture of the technologies and the ways in which they will support the performer. There are four views on setting a leadership stance based on a company's culture.

1) *Performer at the center*
2) *Manager at the center*
3) *Technologies at the center*
4) *Speed at the center*

Performer at the center

Recently, both government and non-governmental organizations have become highly customer-centric, regardless of whether customers are internal or external. I am not debating this topic here because it has advantages.

But, in my research, the companies that drastically sped up employee performance were employee-centric, as shown in Figure 3.2. Their leadership emphasized that employees are the face of the company. They believed that employee abilities and the speed with which they attain the necessary abilities are the critical drivers to better customer service, better business outcomes, sustainable revenues, and higher operational efficiency. Such organizations made the six elements of the ecosystem work in sync to ensure that their employees come up to the required speed faster. Their managers, peers, coaches, mentors, technologies, experts, and the overall work environment were all geared toward one thing—employees' success.

The logic here is that if you measure their proficiency in terms of business KPIs, you automatically address all your business and customer or operational goals in one shot.

Figure 3.2: Keeping performers or employees at the center.

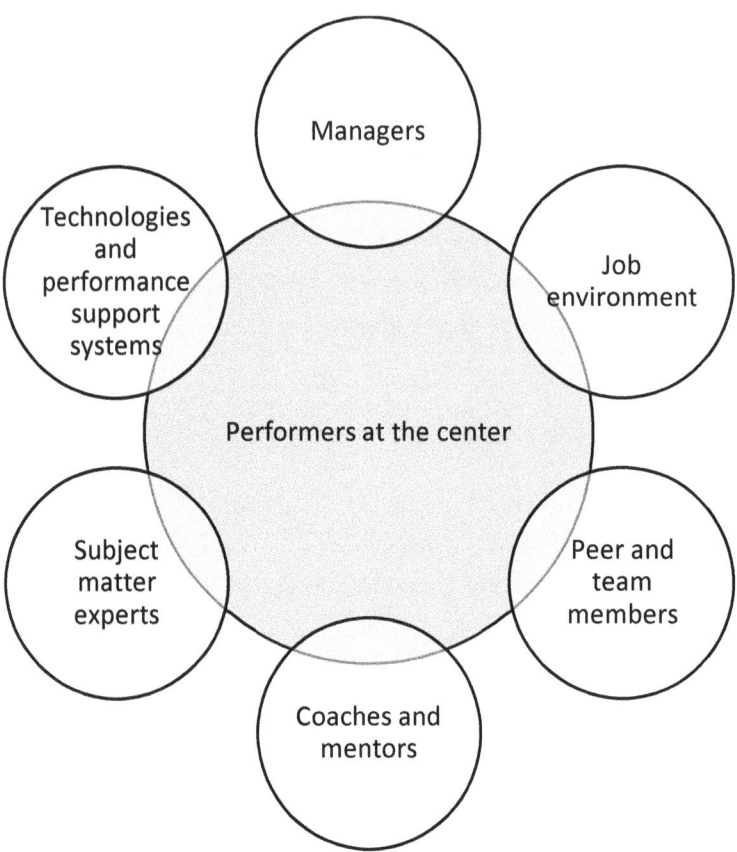

These leaders created an enabling and supportive environment that was specifically designed to let employees know how their speed matters. They specifically focused on the guidance that the employees were getting from their peers. They ensured that they drove a network of coaches to have the right coach for the right employee at every step of the way. They did not say, "Go sit with Jim; if Jim is unavailable, then sit with Joe." Instead, they asked for more structured, more accountable coaching processes in their organizations. They then created the necessary platforms, forums, and meetings to get employees to access the top performers, experts, and subject matter experts (SMEs) in any part of the company so that they could leverage previous organizational knowledge to get faster instead of reinventing the wheel.

These leaders were reasonably tech-savvy to decide what kind of technologies and PSSs they must provide their employees to get them the JIT support at the point of need. I will touch upon this in detail in a while.

The point here is that the moment you, as a leader, keep your performers at the center and make their speed of development as your No. 1 priority, you will start creating a culture in which all elements work together to bring that speed in them.

Now, the question that comes up is, 'Who can make all the things happen in this ecosystem?' To do so, go to the next section, 'Manager at the Center.'

Manager at the center

The most crucial component of the success of the entire ecosystem is the direct frontline managers. If we look at the ecosystem from how the work is actually being done in organizations, we will see that managers are at the center, as shown in Figure 3.3. Managers or leaders are the ones who are responsible for creating resources, relationships, systems, and environments for employees to learn, perform, and develop. They are the ones who give the performance goals. Logically, they are the ones who can help the most to achieve those goals at a faster rate.

The leaders in the best-in-class organizations train and empower their frontline managers with three strategic behaviors that impact TTP drastically.

Figure 3.3: Keeping managers at the center.

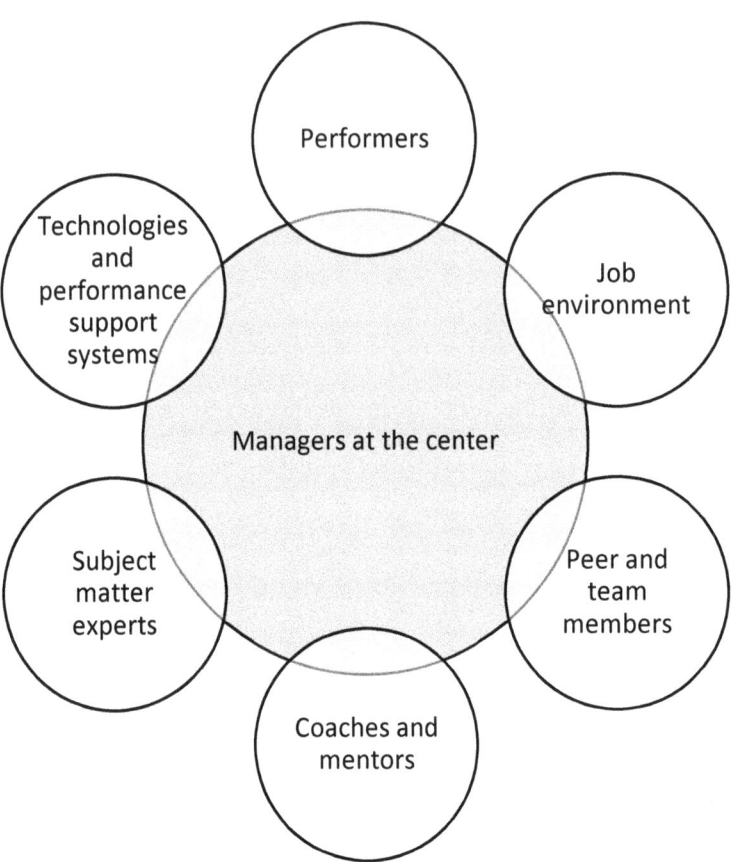

Technologies at the center

In the post-pandemic new normal, you have to think strategically about which technology can support speed and which is for process efficiency only. That puts technology at the center, as shown in Figure 3.4.

3/ STRATEGIC LEARNING TECHNOLOGY LEADERSHIP THINKING

Figure 3.4: Keeping technologies at the center.

In my research, I found that the right kind of technologies, not all kinds of technologies, the right kind of it, tremendously cut out the time from that proficiency journey. The most significant impact on speed-to-proficiency was caused by those called PSSs. In some cases, these new tools can completely replace the need for formal training, and field staff is made to learn on the go. The time-to-readiness is tremendously shortened.

Irrespective of the PSS used by the organization, you, as a learning technologist, need to have a strategic focus on which PSS can eliminate the need for training, which PSS can allow onsite training, which PSS can allow remote assistance, and which PSS can help field staff to access knowledge and experts on the go. But, you need to be fully aware of making sure that the PSSs are integrated into the workflow. If employees are not dependent on PSSs, you will not be able to get their full value on speed-to-proficiency.

Speed at the center

The world is not the same anymore. Amidst the speed of business, you have to focus not only on the speed of employee development but also the speed of technological revolution, speed of product launches, and speed in other aspects of the business.

Once you consider speed in every aspect of business operations, projects, and processes, you have to rethink everything. From hiring to succession planning to organizational design, learning interventions, and leadership strategies—all are focused and designed for speed. That means keeping speed at the center, as shown in Figure 3.5.

If you ride upon that viewpoint today, you will retain a futuristic, competitive, and speed-savvy leadership stance in the coming decade.

3/ STRATEGIC LEARNING TECHNOLOGY LEADERSHIP THINKING

Figure 3.5: Keeping goals for speed at the center.

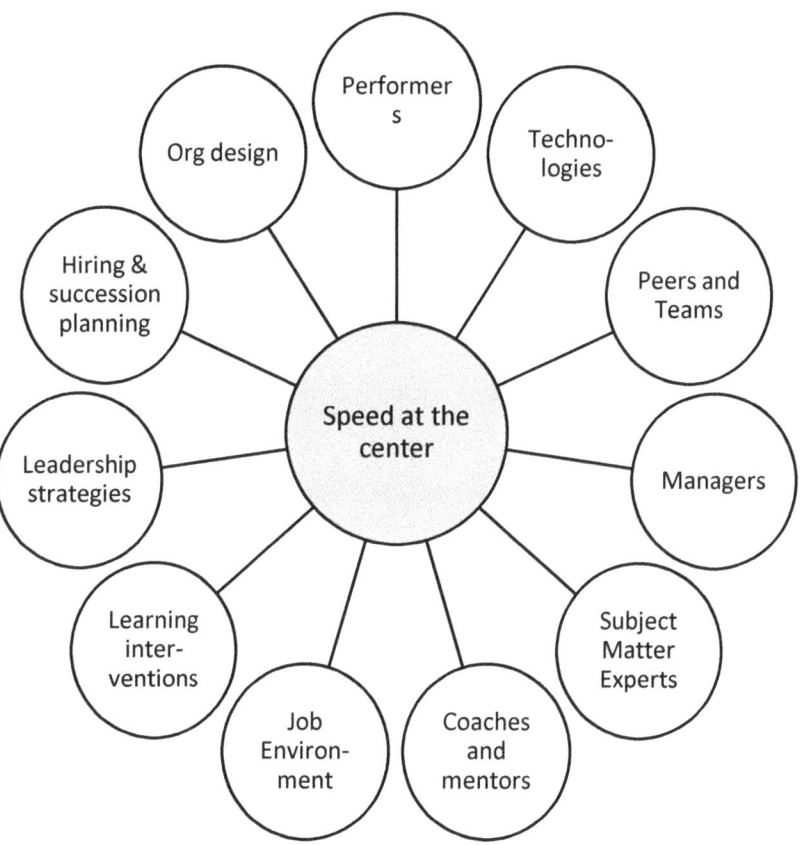

Choosing the right ecosystem

All four ecosystems are equally powerful. It depends upon your organizational strategy.

If your organization focuses highly on employees, you might do well by keeping employees at the center.

If your organizational culture revolves around a lot of empowerment to managers, and they are ultimately held accountable for all the business results, then you might be good with a manager-centric ecosystem.

If you are on the digital transformation wave and prioritize technologies at the heart of corporate strategies, you might be better off implementing a technology-centric ecosystem.

However, there is no doubt that if you want to stay competitive in the market, you better implement a speed-centric ecosystem. In my book *Speed Matters*, I have laid out the science of building speed as your anchor.

Closed-loop system to shorten TTP metrics

You will need a system to integrate all analytics with TTP metrics. There are five general steps. Figure 3.6 shows the five steps.

Step 1: Define proficiency metrics

The first step in setting up analytics is to define proficiency for each job role. For that, you need to establish quantifiable metrics to the extent possible so that data analytics can tell you where your employees are in each job role relative to those metrics.

Step 2: Baseline TTP

The second step is to baseline the TTP for all the employees in a given role. It is easier said than done! An important part of this step is to implement data analytics that allows you to measure the proficiency level of employees at each stage as well as keep computing TTP for those who have attained the required proficiency measures.

3/ STRATEGIC LEARNING TECHNOLOGY LEADERSHIP THINKING

Then, you aggregate across employee groups and job roles to create a baseline number.

The baseline step will tell you how big TTP is and how worrisome it could be for your business. Once you know how big the TTP will be in your settings, you can compute the dollars being burned due to slow TTP very well. The baseline number translates to things like money you are losing, opportunity costs you are missing, customer servicing, or the potential revenue lost. That is how you will assign a dollar value per unit reduction in that TTP.

Figure 3.6: Five-step approach to speed up employee development.

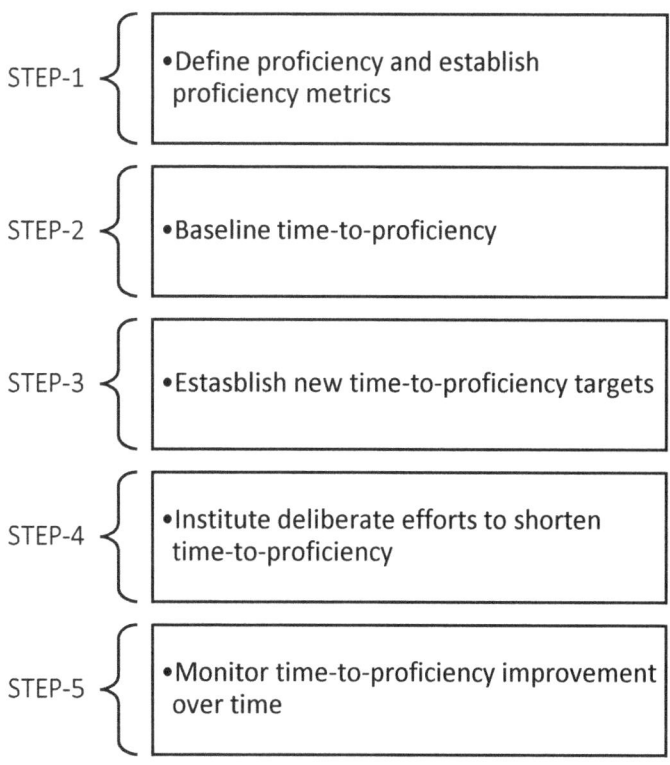

Step 3: Establish TTP targets

Once you are clear about what you want to improve, you will be able to determine the TTP number that needs to be reduced—10%, 20%, or how much? Well....It depends! All you have to do is to assess what is feasible and achievable in your settings. In my research, I noted an up to 80% reduction in TTP.

Step 4: Deliberate efforts

Then comes the phase when you would make deliberate and conscious efforts to drive down the TTP. You will institute projects, initiatives, task force teams, and resources to make deliberate and conscious efforts to reduce the TTP. There are numerous strategies to achieve this reduction.

Step 5: Monitor TTP

The last step ends with monitoring the improvement in TTP. You would use the same set of metrics that you used to establish proficiency metrics and the same mechanism that you used to baseline TTP. If the TTP does not improve as per set targets, you will have to relook at the strategies and systems you put in place.

Strategic thinking for speed of employee development

Let me anchor you back to the proficiency–time graph. I will then map this graph to five speed-focused strategies.

If you look closely at the proficiency–time graph presented in Figure 2.2, you will see five components or determinants of faster employee development, which are shown in Figure 3.7:

3/ STRATEGIC LEARNING TECHNOLOGY LEADERSHIP THINKING

- Zero-point: The initial level of proficiency from which an individual starts his/her journey. The higher the initial level, the better the headstart and the shorter the TTP.
- Horizontal dotted line: The proficiency level that needs to be achieved or demonstrated in a given job. The higher this level is, the longer it will take to reach the required proficiency.
- Normal proficiency curve: The longer the length, the longer the time (T1) to reach the target proficiency line.
- Angles: Angles represent the lifts required for an accelerated proficiency curve to meet the target proficiency line in a shorter time (T2). The higher the lift, the shorter the TTP.
- Time marks: Time marks T1 and T2 indicate relatively how soon someone can reach the target proficiency line.

These five determinants reveal five strategies to speed up employee performance: (1) hiring the right talent; (2) defining specific proficiency metrics; (3) work skills that matter; (4) efficient learning path; and (5) tracking and measuring time.

#1: Hiring the right talent

Suppose you are able to hire the right talent for a job who will bring the same competencies and experience that seasoned employees already possess, then the 'accelerated proficiency curve' can start higher on the proficiency axis. This headstart, hiring at higher proficiency, allows one to reach the desired thresholds quickly.

Thus, you need to strategize technologies and analytics in order for you to hire the right talent. You need to assess the kinds of skills and experience they bring. The more such headstart you create, the shorter the TTP will be.

Figure 3.7: Five determinants of speed of employee development.

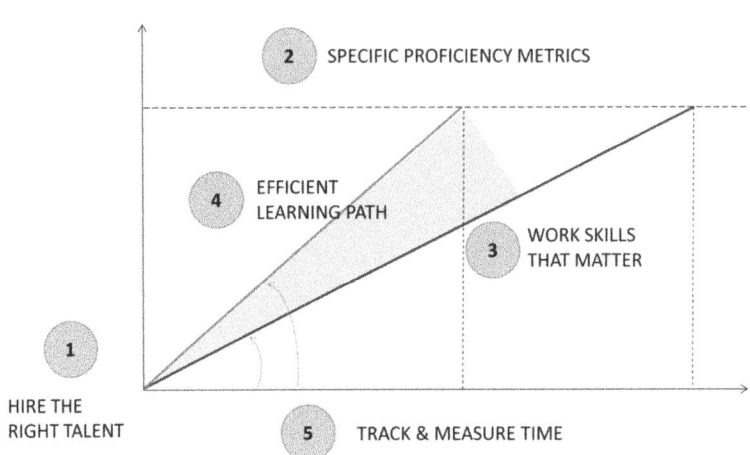

#2: Specific proficiency metrics

The incoming proficiency could be anything, generally out of your hands. The desired proficiency has a pre-defined value. How big the difference between the desired proficiency threshold and the incoming proficiency determines how soon one can close that gap, irrespective of whether one has a headstart or not.

Thus, how the specific proficiency metrics are defined for a job and how the threshold to chase is defined greatly affect the speed with which one can achieve the desired proficiency. If you can strategize technologies and analytics that can accurately measure and track employee proficiency in each job role.

#3: Work skills that matter

The number of work skills required to be learned by employees in a given job has a significant bearing on how long it will take to master them. Thus, it is vital that we accurately identify the work skills that

3/ STRATEGIC LEARNING TECHNOLOGY LEADERSHIP THINKING

matter the most in producing the outcomes that help them achieve proficiency metrics. The key is to focus on the essentials that matter; you will have a shorter time.

Thus, if you can strategize technologies and analytics that can ensure tracking work activities of employees in various situations and perform multilayer analysis on the data to identify trends and patterns, you may be able to ascertain the essential skills and activities required to master that job.

#4: Efficient learning path

The efficiency of the path you give to your employees has a strong bearing on how soon they will be able to reach the target thresholds. If the learning path involves many wasteful activities or irrelevant things that are not contributing toward their ultimate proficiency, you are never going to be able to speed up their journey.

Thus, you need to employ technologies and analytics to design an efficient learning path that focuses only on mastering what really matters. Such an act can make the journey leaner and faster.

#5: Track and measure time

You are implementing all the above to cut and shorten the time from their journey. Thus, the most important anchor is measuring time. You must track and measure time so that you know how much time your employees are taking to reach different points of that journey. Most technologies have time stamps and are invariably able to track time. However, not all technologies or analytics roll those tracking into TTP metrics.

The above five determinants determine the corresponding strategies for technologies and analytics that can ensure the dynamics. These determinants translate into the following five principles. Institute or select the technologies and analytics that can allow you to:

1. Identify the characteristics of work and performers to hire the right talent for a new role.
2. Determine the measures and metrics of job-specific proficiency thresholds across all job roles.
3. Analyze, determine, and limit the skills and content that employees are absolutely required to master.
4. Design, manage, and track a highly efficient and lean learning path for employees.
5. Measure time intervals across a range of events and compute speed.

These five guiding principles become the foundation for your strategic technology leadership framework, as shown in Figure 3.8.

Figure 3.8: Five strategies for technology implementation.

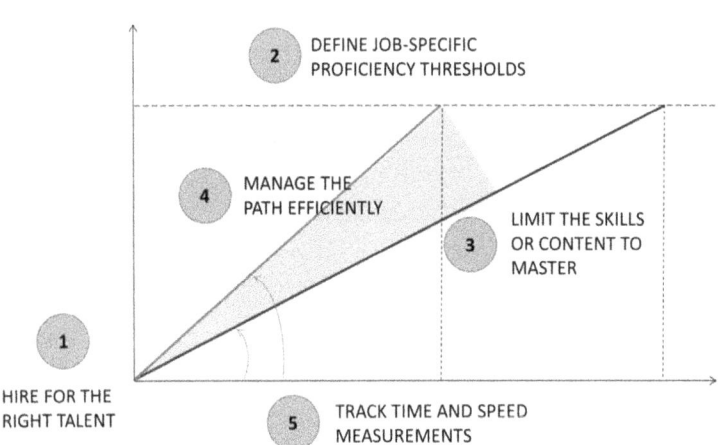

3/ STRATEGIC LEARNING TECHNOLOGY LEADERSHIP THINKING

A simplified representation is shown in Figure 3.9. In the following chapters, I shall expand on each of these elements of this framework.

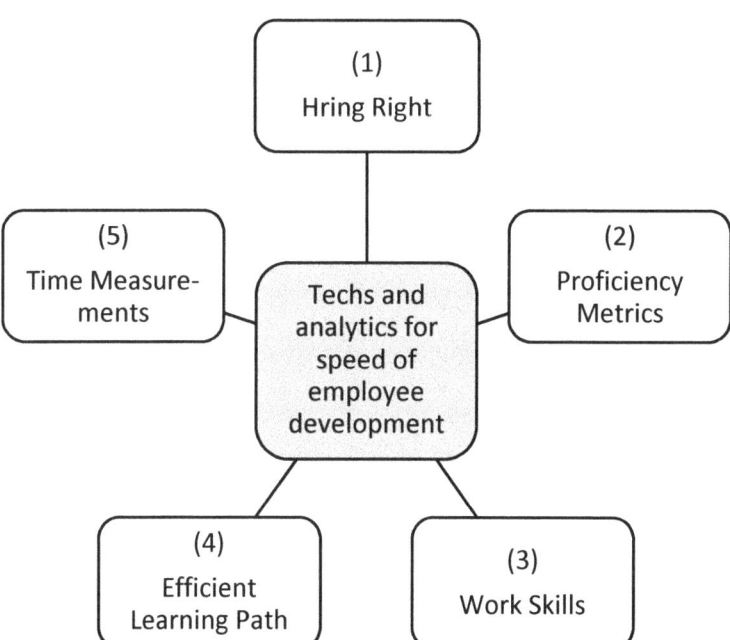

Figure 3.9: Strategic technology thinking framework.

COMPETENCIES FOR STRATEGIC LEARNING TECHNOLOGY LEADERSHIP

I can't emphasize enough as to how strategic thinking is essential to your success. To be more strategic in your position, here are a few competencies you need to acquire:

Master the science of speed in an organization

The need for speed has fueled the growth of various learning technologies and platforms. Thus, as a strategic learning technology leader, the first thing that you need to master is the science of speed. Your job is not thoroughly done until you are fully educated on the strategies for measuring and ensuring speed in organizations. Thus, as the most important aspect of strategic thinking, you need to master the metrics and science behind organizational speed. Above all, you need to learn how to measure your workforce's TTP metrics (see following chapters) and how your learning technologies will improve them.

Measure and report key performance indicators that matter

To be more strategic, a strategic learning technology leader should measure and report the outcomes of learning technology initiatives. This involves identifying key performance indicators (KPIs) for the functions that need to be improved with the help of technologies. You will then need to collect and analyze the KPI data to ascertain that you will invest wisely in the things that matter to the business. Among others, the critical metrics in today's fast-paced world are related to the speed of employee development, such as TTP, time-to-first success, and time-to-market. Unless you keep yourself up to the

3/ STRATEGIC LEARNING TECHNOLOGY LEADERSHIP THINKING

required speed on how to impact these KPIs with e-learning, you will have challenges in making your mark.

Develop a long-term vision for learning technologies in the organization

To be more strategic, you should develop a long-term vision for learning technologies and infrastructure in the organization. This involves looking beyond the organization's immediate needs and identifying how new revolutions can support its future goals and objectives. This is, beyond doubt, the most important aspect because the shelf life of most technologies is low, which also means that the rate of obsolescence is on the rise. Often, learning technology leaders are in a firefighting mode because they do not usually take into account the issues related to obsolescence, sustenance, and upgrading of technology into their roadmaps and budgets. However, using too many technologies is capital-intensive. Thus, obsolescence needs to be computed in depreciation from a financial angle. In addition, you also need to look at how fast you can upgrade and replace the technologies if a vendor declares a technology as 'end-of-support.' Thus, you have to be highly mindful of the impact the replacement of any existing technology can cause. This also means fresh logistics and financial and leadership investment in change management.

Monitor industry trends and best practices

Usually, learning technology professionals tend to spend a lot of energy in trying to convince their senior management about the value of something that has, unfortunately, not proliferated into the market fully but has been tried successfully in some select places. To effectively build strategic thinking, you as a strategic learning technology leader, must stay up-to-date on industry trends and best practices in the learning technology space through forums, conferences, and research reports. This involves monitoring industry publications, attending conferences and events, and networking with other learning tech professionals. This allows you to look beyond your horizon and anticipate changes and the evolution of technologies. Often, learning technology professionals or leaders build roadmaps that look glorious to their executives. But, they hide the bitter truth about what is coming and how soon it needs to be integrated into mainstream operations. You can be preemptive in building roadmaps to stay ready for those changes.

Evaluate emerging e-learning technologies

To be more strategic, stay up-to-date on emerging e-learning platforms and learning technologies, and evaluate their potential to support the organization's L&D goals. This involves looking beyond the currently available technologies and identifying new and innovative ways to use technology to support e-learning, mobile learning, and on-demand performance technologies. This can be a tricky area as reading reports or best-known methods alone will not give you the confidence that what works in another organization will work in yours as well. You have to do a pilot and test the integration with other infrastructural elements of the company. However, this does invite massive investment! Most business executives responsible for revenues are only interested in knowing the Return on Investment (ROI) of experimental technology investments. There is no easy answer. You should be able to conduct your experimentation inside or outside your organization. Being a part of a research body, group of university researchers, or start-ups is a great way to execute such evaluations flawlessly. You can explore how to set up tie-offs with emerging start-ups and give them fair play to test out their technology while you focus on how the same can help you achieve your organizational goals.

3/ STRATEGIC LEARNING TECHNOLOGY LEADERSHIP THINKING

Align learning technology strategy with overall business strategy

To be more strategic, you should conduct regular needs assessments to determine the organization's learning needs. This involves identifying the skills and knowledge that learners need to acquire in order to succeed. You will then need to identify whether there are gaps in the organization's current learning platforms or technologies in terms of developing employees efficiently. At the end, you need to ensure that your e-learning strategy aligns with the organization's overall business strategy.

TAKING IT FORWARD

In this chapter, you learned a leadership framework for making the right decisions for learning technology implementation in an organization. You learned that you need to focus on employee development and consider them as people rather than resources or things. This chapter culminated with five strategies for identifying, implementing, and strategizing technologies for shortening the TTP of employees. In the following chapter, you will learn the first strategy to implement technologies and analytics for hiring the right talent.

Use the space below to reflect upon and note down your major takeaways to this point.

STRATEGIC LEARNING TECHNOLOGY LEADERSHIP

Reflections 3.1

Chapter 1
DIGITAL REVOLUTION IN LEARNING TECHNOLOGIES

Chapter 2
BUSINESS KPIs FOR LEARNING TECHNOLOGY

Chapter 3
STRATEGIC LEARNING TECHNOLOGY LEADERSHIP THINKING

Chapter 4
TECHNOLOGIES & ANALYTICS FOR HIRING RIGHT

Chapter 5
TECHNOLOGIES & ANALYTICS FOR PROFICIENCY METRICS

Chapter 6
TECHNOLOGIES & ANALYTICS FOR WORK SKILLS

Chapter 7
TECHNOLOGIES & ANALYTICS FOR EFFICIENT LEARNING PATH

Chapter 8
TECHNOLOGIES & ANALYTICS FOR TIME MEASUREMENTS

Chapter 9
EMERGING TECHNOLOGIES FOR SPEED

Chapter 10
THE FINAL THOUGHTS

BONUS
MODELLING GEN-AI FOR ENTERPRSE L&D

L&D CAREER RESOURCES

4

TECHNOLOGIES & ANALYTICS FOR HIRING RIGHT

4/ TECHNOLOGIES AND ANALYTICS FOR HIRING RIGHT

The first parameter on the proficiency–time graph is the starting point of the curves. That determines speed! People bring some level of skills or mastery to the new roles for which they are hired. Hiring the right incoming people with successful behaviors, skills, and competencies similar to those seasoned employees who came up-to speed faster in the past will give you a headstart. The end result is that they take a shorter time to reach the target proficiency level.

The first strategy pertains to technologies and analytics that could help to hire the right talent. Such technologies and analytics should allow you to identify and profile the skills of people you are bringing into a new role and be able to determine their proficiency level at the hiring stage.

LOOK BEYOND BASIC DATA

When hiring new employees, you typically use specific data before, during, and after hiring. Organizations often look for HR technologies or analytics, which is all about the process efficiency of hiring or managing employee data. Most talent analytics measures track the overall health of recruitment strategies and measure performance over things like candidate source, time-to-fill, and cost-per-hire. From a HR standpoint, recruiters gather data such as education profile, diversity distribution, age distribution, retention ratio, average service time, time to hire, and compensation comparison. Such data have no meaning or contribution toward shortening TTP, other than meeting the operational obligation of running a department.

In order to build faster TTP, you need to look for something beyond those factors.

STRATEGIC LEARNING TECHNOLOGY LEADERSHIP

TECHNOLOGIES FOR PERFORMER PROFILING

The management of a large oil & gas company faced the challenge of long TTPs of its console operators, who were in charge of pump operations onboard petroleum extraction stations. The TTP was of the order of 24 weeks. Imagine that the management has to wait for 6 months for their operators to come up-to the desired speed. This means a loss of both productivity and revenue. Every extra minute that they spend onboard in the sea being unproductive costs the company more money.

So, the management thought that they needed to do something about it. First, they identified those operators from their historical data who reached the required performance in a shorter time. They deployed feedback systems, cameras, and observers to watch them working. They then deployed some experts to watch those employees and understand what they were doing differently compared to the rest of the operators. By doing this, the management found that the few employees who were star performers looked at monitors, and, instead of touching the controls on a specified console, would go to a specific place on the process floor and finetune the required valves. However, this was not the standard operating procedure (SOP). It turned out that these few guys had figured out a way to precisely know which valve to finetune downstream based on the parameters on the screen. Surprisingly, such a skill was never considered a requirement for the job.

From that point onwards, they started hiring or developing their operators with that kind of process analysis skills and some ability to assess physical parameters. The result was a drastic reduction in TTP of new operators.

4/ TECHNOLOGIES AND ANALYTICS FOR HIRING RIGHT

The key thing that came out of that analytics is that they could then investigate how those star performers have got ahead of the curve. Are they following the entire procedure, or have they developed their own best-known methods? What if we give those success behaviors that sped up star performers to everyone in the workforce? So, that content goes into training to improve everyone's TTP.

This is an old project case, but now several organizations are using the latest technologies that could allow you to use a range of analytics on employee activities to do behavior or skills analysis to identify successful behaviors. It creates a hiring profile of the ideal candidates, like what kind of experience or skills they should possess.

There are three things to consider:

1. ***Success behavior of star players***
2. ***Skills or behaviors to hire for***
3. ***Accurate job mapping***

1. Technologies to analyze success behaviors of star performers

An article by Harvard Business Review suggests that using analytics to track employee behavior can help identify top performers and better understand the factors that drive productivity.

Organizations deploy various technologies to profile their employees' skills, expertise, and capabilities. But, it is primarily hiring-focused and promotion-focused and serves only the HR department—well, mostly!

However, some organizations do annual surveys or assessments of their employees' skills. Some even track the behaviors they display to bring out the outcomes. Such technologies aim to identify your star performers who have shown a shorter TTP. Once you identify them, you can then figure out what they do differently. Perhaps you could teach some of those behaviors to the remaining workforce to accelerate them as well.

Technologies for creating hiring profiles

Several organizations have the latest profiling technologies that centralize all information about employees' roles, responsibilities, and performance with their own skill additions. However, they need something more to capture and log employees' transactional and project performance, like major wins and results. Apart from that, they also have to have their activity logs and measurements, such as TTP, time-to-productivity, and time to certification. When matched with correct analytics, leaders can perform a range of analyses on employee activities, behaviors, or skills to identify the patterns and trends of success behaviors that result in their performance at an accelerated rate. These success behaviors are then used to create a hiring profile of the ideal candidates, such as experience, skills, expertise, and background required to perform that job. The idea of creating such a profile is to hire employees with similar competencies so that there is a high probability of being a star performer in a shorter time.

One such example is ActivTrak[3], which does such monitoring. ActivTrak is a workforce analytics and productivity monitoring tool that helps organizations gain insights into employee performance and engagement. By collecting and analyzing data on employee activities, behaviors, and skillsets, ActivTrak enables employers to

---

[3] ActivTrack. Employee Monitor Software. https://www.activtrak.com/solutions/employee-monitoring/

create detailed hiring profiles that align with the specific requirements of their organization. Companies using ActivTrak have reported improved employee productivity and reduced TTP, ultimately leading to higher overall business success.

The People Analytics team at Google[4] has been a pioneer in using data-driven approaches to inform their hiring processes. The team analyzed large amounts of data on employee performance, productivity, and tenure to identify patterns that indicate success in various roles (Bock, 2015). By incorporating these findings into their hiring profiles, Google has been able to attract candidates who are more likely to thrive in the company culture and contribute significantly to the organization's success.

Another example in a similar category is AI-powered IBM Watson Talent Frameworks, discussed in the previous section.

Technologies to conduct cluster analysis

Some analytics support cluster analysis, which allows group employees based on specific characteristics or behaviors. For example, an employer could use cluster analysis to group employees based on their sales performance, outcomes, productivity, project success, or customer satisfaction, to identify trends and patterns. By grouping employees based on these factors, organizations can pinpoint high performers and implement strategies to replicate their success. In a case study[5], cluster analysis was used to identify high-performing shipment professionals in a delivery company; the work behaviors or preferences of these professionals were identified. In

---

[4]Bock, L. (2015). Work Rules!: Insights from Inside Google That Will Transform How You Live and Lead. Hachette Books.
[5]Estrada-Cedeno et. al. 2019. The Good, the Bad and the Ugly: Workers Profiling through Clustering Analysis. https://www.researchgate.net/publication/332291665

another study[6], researchers identified self-leadership as key to individual innovation among hospital nurses.

Salesforce[7] analytics products like customer relationship management (CRM) Analytics and Einstein AI for Tableau are examples of platforms that allow organizations to analyze large amounts of data and uncover valuable insights. They use cluster analysis which can group employees based on various factors such as sales performance, customer engagement, and geographical location. By identifying star performers, organizations can gain a better understanding of the characteristics that contribute to high performance and develop targeted training and development programs to help other employees reach their full potential.

For instance, Tableau[8] can conduct cluster analysis and advanced data visualization to cluster customer service representatives based on their performance metrics. This can help companies identify the best practices of top-performing employees and apply them across their organizations. Similarly, Microsoft[9] PowerBI, an advanced business analytics platform, can be used to conduct cluster analysis on employee data. The tool allows employees to be grouped based on sales performance and customer feedback. The analysis can reveal the specific behaviors and strategies employed by top performers that contribute to their success. Companies can then use the information to develop training programs aimed at improving the performance of their new employees.

---

[6] Gomes C et. Al. 2015. Better Off together: A cluster analysis of self-leadership and its relationship to individual innovation in hospital nurses. Psicologia. Vol. 29 (1), 45-58.
https://core.ac.uk/download/pdf/302955271.pdf
[7] https://www.salesforce.com/products/analytics/overview/?d=cta-body-promo-32
[8] https://www.tableau.com/
[9] https://powerbi.com

4/ TECHNOLOGIES AND ANALYTICS FOR HIRING RIGHT

Technologies to conduct factor analysis

Powerful analytics technologies allow organizations to use decision-tree analysis to identify patterns or relationships in employee data. For example, an employer could use decision-tree analysis to determine which factors are most important in predicting an employee's job performance, such as their education level, years of experience, or job responsibilities. This can help identify critical success factors in hiring a new workforce with similar characteristics.

A job hunting company[10] was able to use IBM SPSS Decision Trees, a powerful analytical tool, to identify key factors and relationships in their data, such as education level, years of experience, and job responsibilities. By identifying the most critical factors predicting job performance, the company was able to refine its hiring processes for its clients to target candidates with similar characteristics, leading to higher levels of employee productivity and retention.

As another instance, advanced analytics from RapidMiner[11] platform can help companies analyze employee performance data such as sales figures, customer satisfaction, and job responsibilities. The decision-tree analysis of this data can reveal the key factors contributing to employee success, enabling the company to refine its hiring and training strategies to attract and develop top performers.

Technologies to conduct regression analysis

The RapidMiner can be coupled with regression analysis, which can be used to estimate the relationship between a set of variables. For example, an employer could use regression analysis to determine if

---

[10] IBM (n.d.), Job Master. https://www.ibm.com/case-studies/jobmaster-talent-solutions-recruitment-assessment
[11] RapidMiner. https://rapidminer.com/

there is a relationship between an employee's specific experience and his/her current job performance. If there is a strong relationship, the organization may consider hiring new people with that success parameter.

Several statistical analysis platforms support regression analysis, such as SAS Analytics, Stata, and R Project. They have reported case studies and journal studies indicating how several organizations used strong relationships between employee performance and other variables to refine their hiring process to target candidates with similar experience. In other cases, they provided an identical ecosystem to the new hires to ensure success like seasoned employees. For instance, a technology company used R[12] to analyze the relationship between employee training hours and job performance. The regression analysis revealed a strong positive relationship, indicating that employees with more extensive training performed better in their roles. As a result, the organization invested in more comprehensive training programs for new hires.

2. Technologies to assess candidate skills and behaviors

Once you know the success behaviors that you need for an employee to be proficient at a faster rate, you will hire new candidates for those exact behaviors. That can give an organization a headstart in terms of needing less time to develop. This also means that you can identify who produces results and can coach new people to induct the right behaviors.

---

[12]Smith, J., & Jones, M. (2022). The impact of employee training on job performance: A regression analysis. Journal of Workplace Learning, 34(1), 45-60.

4/ TECHNOLOGIES AND ANALYTICS FOR HIRING RIGHT

Deloitte's 2018 Global Human Capital Trends survey[13] found that the use of workforce data to analyze, predict, and improve performance had exploded in practice and importance over the last few years. Employee analytics, also known as people analytics, is the use of data analysis techniques to gain insights into an organization's workforce, including hiring, retention, and employee engagement.

Technologies for candidate profiling and screening

The first step of hiring is to analyze the resumes, candidate profiles, and experience. AI-based technologies are revolutionizing the hiring process by automating some of those tasks, reducing bias, improving candidate experience, and providing personalized recommendations. Organizations and recruiters who use these tools can find the right talent for the right job more efficiently and effectively.

Some technologies like JANZZ[14] use AI to parse candidate resumes, do automated classification, semantic extraction, and job or skill categorization, and run several analyses.

Another tool, Ideal[15], uses AI to automatically match candidates with job requirements, providing a list of top candidates. This enables recruiters to shortlist accurately and screen resumes more fairly.

Intel recently reported using an AI-powered algorithm from HiredScore[16] to perform automated matching of its job posting to the candidate database the company has stored for years. It helped recruiters to automatically analyze various data points, including

---

[13] Deloitte. 2018 Global Human Capital Trends.
https://www2.deloitte.com/content/dam/Deloitte/uk/Documents/human-capital/deloitte-uk-human-capital-trends-2018.pdf
[14] JANZZ Technology. https://janzz.technology/
[15] Ideal. S&P Data increased retention by 20%. https://ideal.com/customer/sp-data/
[16] Karp, A. (n.d.). HiredScore. The Rise of Talent Intelligence. Talent Tech Labs.
https://www.hiredscore.com/resources?type=Case+Studies

resumes and social media profiles. Intel used the capabilities of this software to hire 150 candidates from their current database.

Technologies for pre-hire assessments

The popularity of pre-hire assessments is growing among companies that want more predictive accuracy in their hiring processes. These assessments use employee analytics to provide insights into a candidate's potential job performance based on his/her skills, personality, and cognitive abilities. Some even use psychometric testing technologies to evaluate a candidate's cognitive skills, personality traits, and mental capabilities to determine the extent to which they match the job requirements.

HireVue[17] used AI in video interviewing to analyze candidates' facial expressions, tone of voice, and language to assess their skills, personality, and cultural fit. This assessment platform enabled recruiters to identify and hire the best talent quickly.

An American call center company used a tool called Modern Hire[18] to virtually hire their call center candidates while predicting which candidate can ensure higher retention. The technology allowed them to assess a candidate's fit and his/her feel for what the job entailed. Candidates engaged in exercises that measured their situational judgment and ability to multitask. The result was that the right candidates were put in the job. It was seen that the top 30% of the candidates hired so were three times more likely to have a higher performance rating.

---

[17] https://www.hirevue.com/
[18] Modern Hire. Assessing Candidates for Call Center Customer Service Roles. https://modernhire.com/call-center-customer-service/

4/ TECHNOLOGIES AND ANALYTICS FOR HIRING RIGHT

Predictive analytics

Another powerful method is using predictive analytics to analyze data on an employee's past performance and skills to predict their future success in a particular role. These assessments consider various factors such as personality traits, cognitive ability, and work style and help companies make more informed hiring decisions.

A leading hospitality company implemented predictive assessments in its recruitment process. The assessments evaluated candidates on their job-related knowledge, problem-solving ability, and customer service skills. This helped the company identify top-performing candidates and match them to the job roles where they are most likely to excel. As a result, the company has seen a 94% retention rate for new hires and improved customer satisfaction scores.

Another company in the healthcare and wellness products sector used predictive assessments to evaluate candidates for their graduate program. The assessments measured the candidates' potential and suitability for the program by evaluating their cognitive ability, personality, and values. This has helped the company identify those candidates who are most likely to succeed in the program and contribute to the company's success.

3. Technologies for accurate job mapping

Once you have identified the star performers' difference-making behaviors and made it your mandate to hire people with similar characteristics, you can be certain that your hiring process is lined up with what already works. That way, you can match the right people to the right job. This simple action accelerates proficiency tremendously when the right skills are applied to the right job—you don't have to learn anything new.

Technologies for internal employee profiling

An employee profile is a tool that helps companies find and hire the right people, especially in fast-growing companies. It contains personal information, work history, skills, and other details that make it easier for managers to assign projects and training.

Some organizations use technology to analyze workforce data and identify which candidates are the most likely to be successful in a given job role. By doing so, they can improve their employee retention rates and achieve their business objectives faster and in a more effective manner.

For instance, Chevron[19], an American Oil & Gas corporation, used Eightfold AI algorithms to match the skills and experience of the existing employees with open positions within the organization. They used their HR data stored in WorkDay platform to identify their internal employees' skills, capabilities, and past achievements and then matched them to the job postings. They effectively transformed traditional recruiters into career advisors, massively reducing time-to-fill.

Technologies to access a wider pool of talent

In the past, recruitment was limited to local candidates or those who were willing to relocate. However, today's recruitment technology allows hiring managers to access a wider pool of candidates from around the world. Some platforms like Topcoder or Kaggle allow companies to post projects and tap into a global network of skilled

---

[19] Albinus, P. (2021). How Chevron Drilled into Its HR Data to Tap New Talent. https://hrexecutive.com/how-chevron-drilled-into-its-hr-data-to-tap-new-talent/

4/ TECHNOLOGIES AND ANALYTICS FOR HIRING RIGHT

freelancers. This gives recruiters a better chance of finding the right talent for the job. Companies can make more informed hiring decisions and better match candidates to job roles. This can lead to improved employee retention, higher job satisfaction, and better business outcomes.

Technologies for post-hiring matching analysis

Some workforce management systems allow detailed analytics to perform incoming candidates' skills and behavioral profiling. The idea is to match candidates to the right role and put them at the right point in that proficiency trajectory, regardless of the position advertised. It is important to know how people's profiles fit into the job and what traits, experience, and skills can add to that speed. For instance, Eightfold AI uses AI algorithms to match the skills and experience of existing employees with open positions within an organization. This can help reduce the cost and time required to recruit new employees.

Technologies for assessing the perfect job-fit

However, getting the ideal candidates who match the profiles is not always possible. What do you do in that case? Often, those who do not map well to the job being advertised are rejected. However, leaders can follow a different thinking process, which involves engaging great candidates and either putting them in the right job or customizing new job descriptions to fit the candidate's skills.

Google's People Analytics team is a great example[20]. They changed the company's hiring process by using data-driven insights to match candidates with suitable roles (Davenport, 2013)[21]. This

---

[20] Maier S. (2016). How Google Uses People Analytics to Create a Great Workplace. Entreprenuer. https://www.entrepreneur.com/growing-a-business/how-google-uses-people-analytics-to-create-a-great-workplace/284550

[21] https://www.ciosummits.com/media/solution_spotlight/106462_0713.pdf

approach enabled Google to reduce their time to hire, improve employee satisfaction, and save millions of dollars in training and post-hiring investments.

As mentioned earlier, IBM's Watson Talent Frameworks aids organizations in identifying the perfect job-fit candidates by analyzing their skills, experience, and potential.

McKinsey & Company[22] has mentioned the success story of a healthcare organization in one of its articles. One of their clients was undergoing a massive transformation. They had to assess and consider more than 2000 high-potential employees for more than 100 critical positions. The company built a unique competency model tailored toward its values by identifying the 45 most vital value-adding roles and defining markers for success supported by people analytics. The point of this case is not to fill people against open positions but to put the right person into the job. However, being a big hassle, most recruiting managers don't usually take that pain. The reason is that the recruitment department is worried about their KPIs for hiring time and other things.

Traditional methods lead to millions of dollars of training and post-hiring investment that can be avoided by putting people into jobs that best fit their skills, exposure, and experience. That will shorten TTP and save millions of dollars while keeping a competitive edge. That's where technologies like McKinsey's Talent Match come in handy for aggregating data and supporting recommendations. "The tool helped one client develop a company-wide database of high potentials—identifying future leaders, enabling talent mobility, and highlighting top candidates for each job."

---

[22]Breschi, R., Carlin, D., & Schaininger, B. (2018). Matching the right talent to the right roles.
https://www.mckinsey.com/capabilities/people-and-organizational-performance/our-insights/the-organization-blog/matching-the-right-talent-to-the-right-roles

4/ TECHNOLOGIES AND ANALYTICS FOR HIRING RIGHT

Remember that the goal of any perfect-fit job mapping is the fastest possible TTP. Think about this—How often do your HR department or your recruitment managers ask you about the target TTP of the job role you are hiring for? In my experience, hardly ever! They are still using outdated KPIs that are disconnected from the actual business needs.

TAKING IT FORWARD

In this chapter, you learned the first strategy and its considerations for implementing technologies to help organizations hire the right people. You discovered that such a strategy allows companies to shorten TTP faster, giving employees a headstart.

In the next chapter, you will learn the second strategy of the strategic leadership framework to identify and track proficiency metrics.

Use the space below to reflect upon and note down your major takeaways to this point. Among other things you should reflect upon: are you hiring for speed? Once you ask that question, you will see that several people analytics can help you make better-informed decisions about their hiring practices and better match candidates to job roles.

STRATEGIC LEARNING TECHNOLOGY LEADERSHIP

Reflections 4.1

Chapter 1
DIGITAL REVOLUTION IN LEARNING TECHNOLOGIES

Chapter 2
BUSINESS KPIs FOR LEARNING TECHNOLOGY

Chapter 3
STRATEGIC LEARNING TECHNOLOGY LEADERSHIP THINKING

Chapter 4
TECHNOLOGIES & ANALYTICS FOR HIRING RIGHT

Chapter 5
TECHNOLOGIES & ANALYTICS FOR PROFICIENCY METRICS

Chapter 6
TECHNOLOGIES & ANALYTICS FOR WORK SKILLS

Chapter 7
TECHNOLOGIES & ANALYTICS FOR EFFICIENT LEARNING PATH

Chapter 8
TECHNOLOGIES & ANALYTICS FOR TIME MEASUREMENTS

Chapter 9
EMERGING TECHNOLOGIES FOR SPEED

Chapter 10
THE FINAL THOUGHTS

BONUS
MODELLING GEN-AI FOR ENTERPRSE L&D

L&D CAREER RESOURCES

5

TECHNOLOGIES & ANALYTICS FOR PROFICIENCY METRICS

5/ TECHNOLOGIES AND ANALYTICS FOR PROFICIENCY METRICS

No matter whom you hire, you must bring them to an end state of proficiency threshold. If you have a way to measure that end state, if you have a way to know if you are there yet or not or how far your employees are from that state, you will be able to figure out the right strategies to get them there faster. For that, you need to have technologies and analytics to establish the correct thresholds and then be able to track employee progress toward them.

THRESHOLD PROFICIENCY METRICS

How do we know whether employees are anything close to being proficient? Or how do we know where exactly they are on that path?

For this, first, define and establish the desired proficiency thresholds in any job that employees should chase. You must choose performance metrics to measure employee proficiency in a given job. Performance metrics are KPIs that benchmark and measure employee performance, providing insights to them on their contribution and goal achievement in the organization. That includes performance, productivity, and other on-the-job performance indicators.

Such KPIs can provide insights into business conditions such as predictability, early ROI, product quality, and more. However, they need to be measured at the employee level as well as the departmental level.

Choosing the right proficiency metrics

Ideally, you would choose something that makes better sense for the job and business and is also practically achievable. There has to be evidence that employees have achieved it in the past, which has resulted in business benefits. If you do not have such evidence, then it will become improbable for employees to achieve it, irrespective of the best technology you employ.

The metrics you choose for a job must matter to the business's bottom line, and they must convey the achievement of proficiency in that business context. This can be ensured by linking proficiency definitions and metrics to the business metrics for their job roles. You can call these survival metrics because this is how organizations know where their employees stand.

An example of a salesperson's proficiency metrics

Let us take the example of a sales function.

If you want to focus on operation aspects, then you may measure the proficiency of the salesperson as 100 sales closures minimum per month. You will then put all the analytics to track the number of sales, while revenue or the actual value of sales may be secondary data.

If you are a financially driven organization, your proficiency metrics may be a minimum $200K profit per sale. Any profit less than that is not deemed proficient. In this case, you will put analytics to tell you how far you are off on that slated profit.

If you are a strategic organization, perhaps you will want to measure salespeople for market share. In that case, measures would be how many diverse customers they went to and how many more customers were added to the company.

Depending upon your business, you would choose something that makes better sense for the job and business and is also practically achievable.

An example of a service engineer's proficiency metrics

Let us take the example of the photocopier repair technician. How would you measure his proficiency in terms of what matters?

Some possible metrics depend upon whether an organization is more operational, financial, or strategically focused, summarized in Figure 5.1.

An operations-focused organization could use operational metrics such as customer calls per month; cases closed; onsite hours; time on the case; mean time to repair (MTTR); economy of parts used; billable hours; customer satisfaction scores; and first-time-right resolution.

On the other hand, a finance-focused organization could use metrics that deal with money, such as expenses per case; part usage; labor cost; contract margin; and service profit.

Similarly, a strategy-focused organization could use metrics focused on market-based factors and performance such as revenue per customer; revenue by region; revenue per technician; contract reach; Y-o-Y customer sat improvement; and balance scorecard.

Irrespective of the metrics organizations choose based on their business strategies, the same metrics need to be applied to consistently measure the performance and proficiency of technicians.

Figure 5.1: Metrics to measure the proficiency of a repair technician.

Operational	Financial	Strategic
• Customer calls per month • Cases closed • Onsite hours • Time on the case • Mean time to repair • Economy of parts used • Billable hours • Customer sat scores • First time right resolution	• Expenses per case • Part usage • Labor cost • Contract Margin • Service profit	• Revenue per customer • Revenue by region • Revenue per technician • Contract reach • Y-o-Y customer sat improvement • Balance score card

Proficiency metrics based on case closure or handling:

- How quickly s/he spotted the problem?
- How fast s/he fixed the problem?
- How many parts or hours s/he used to fix it?
- What was the customer satisfaction score for the case?
- What was the MTTR in this case?

One way to define using this approach is like this—*100 cases closed per month consistently over a minimum 6 months period.* In this case, you could measure proficiency in terms of when the employee delivers the agreed-upon minimum number of cases, say 100, closed per month,

5/ TECHNOLOGIES AND ANALYTICS FOR PROFICIENCY METRICS

which should be consistent for 6 months at least. The number may have come from certain business goals.

Proficiency metrics based on aggregated monthly output:

- How many cases did s/he solve in a month?
- What is the MTTR across all the cases s/he solved?
- What is the part expenses/economy across all cases?

One way to define using this approach is like this—*MTTR<10 hours consistently over 100 cases*. In another organization, you could measure proficiency of the same job role to see when they deliver you an agreed MTTR over a fairly significant number of cases, say 100.

The point here is that how you define proficiency for any job role directly impacts what data analytics you employ and how you use them to track TTP.

Types of proficiency indicators

In my research, I found 15 indicators of proficiency measurement, which were then grouped into three categories representing the type of proficiency measure:

(1) measurable business outcomes;

(2) observable actions; and

(3) controlled performance.

The list with examples is shown in Table 1.1. Most project leaders defined and measured proficiency of a job role in terms of measurable business outcomes (such as meeting customer satisfaction) or in terms of those observable actions (such as work-output meeting the specifications) that closely represented the business outcomes.

However, in any case, there was not always one single indicator for measuring proficiency. On average, project cases showed that proficiency was measured using two or three different indicators, while business outcomes-related indicators were invariably the primary measurements. For example, the proficiency of customer service executives selling investment products over the phone was measured using three different indicators. Table 6-1 summarizes the three main categories of proficiency measures and their indicators.

But one has to keep in mind that not all jobs are quantifiable. Certain jobs can only be measured with observable actions or behaviors, which an auditor or supervisor can validate, such as the number of action items closed or proposals presented and accepted in the first attempt. An example of such a job would be a manager's job.

Some jobs do not have direct measurements, or it is impossible to measure them in real. For instance, for a firefighter, the metrics could be the number of fires put out. However, this is not something people would wish to have more. Instead, metrics can be their performance in a controlled environment such as a simulated setting.

Therefore, the technology, analytics, and systems must be instituted to capture the metrics based on the nature of the job. But the utmost importance is defining correct proficiency metrics and indicators that suggest if someone has reached that level.

5/ TECHNOLOGIES AND ANALYTICS FOR PROFICIENCY METRICS

Table 1.1: Categories and indicators of proficiency

Type of proficiency measures	Indicator of proficiency	Example
Measurable business outcomes	Business results	All deliveries are on time
		Number of actual sales
		Monthly commissions generated
	Customer satisfaction scores	Customer satisfaction score of 90% or higher
	KPIs improvements	Outages corrected within 1 hour
	Performance specs	Product material within 1% of the specifications
	Productivity	Produce 20 parts to the standards specified by supervisors
Observable actions	Quality and quantity of activities	Number of referrals received
		Number of contacts made
		Success rate in getting new appointments
		Number of action items closed
	Comparison to experienced performers	Within 80% of the metrics shown by a proficient agent
	Evidence from authentic work	Accuracy authenticated by quality assurance auditors
	Number of repetitions	10 repetitions of the task
	Verifiable, observable behaviors	Successful approval of proposals within one attempt
	% of skills mastered	70% of the skills listed on the matrix

Controlled performance	Pre- and post-performance in training	Improvement in pre- and post-testing
	Proficiency scores	X number of points accumulated within 3 months
	Simulated performance	Number of simulations or total time taken to attain the required mastery in the simulator
	Testing at regular intervals	Pass recurring quarterly assessment

DECIDING THE PROFICIENCY MEASUREMENT APPROACH

One of the key things to keep in mind is that there is no one technology that can measure proficiency for all domains. Thus, the technology that you will implement is in the context of the job and the outcomes. That also means that you may have to consider multiple technologies to measure proficiency across all the job roles in your organization. For instance, the technology/technologies that you require to measure the proficiency of technical staff will be different from those required to measure the proficiency of people in the roles of managers.

A feasible workaround to this wide spectrum is to consider framing a strategy or philosophy on how you will measure proficiency across the board. One organization may decide to implement a WorkDay (HR platform) kind of organizational performance system to measure proficiency via performance objectives, while another may resort to using activity-based CRM systems to track the proficiency of employees on a daily basis. Some

5/ TECHNOLOGIES AND ANALYTICS FOR PROFICIENCY METRICS

organizations may decide to implement SalesForce kind of systems to measure proficiency in terms of outcomes. The bottom line is that you have to decide how you are measuring proficiency in each job role versus across the organization. Such a decision has a profound and far-reaching impact on how proficiency measurement technologies are implemented.

TECHNOLOGIES AND ANALYTICS

Depending upon your chosen metrics and the proficiency measurement approach, you need technologies and analytics to measure them precisely and do extensive analysis to stay on top of them. The idea is to have technologies or analytics that can tell you whether or not employees are producing the results for which they are hired—things like their outputs, business results, successes, productivity, and other KPIs. Part of this is also to include analytics that can tell you proficiency at the employee, group, or role level.

You could be chasing the wrong thresholds if you don't use proper technologies that are in line with your metrics. For instance, if you choose to track the number of cold calls made, all your salespersons maybe star players making endless calls but not putting up enough revenue because you implemented tracking systems in place to measure things that did not matter. In such cases, you will run into a situation where you will not hold them accountable for the same.

Leveraging CRM and ERP technologies

To chase the correct thresholds, most organizations employ two technologies—customer relationship management (CRM) and employee resource processing (ERP)—irrespective of the business sector or company. While CRM deals with what happens with customers, like contracts, revenues, sales, engagement, and service, ERP deals with the company's overall financial and operational data. Some famous ones are SAP, Zoho, SalesForce, and Oracle.

These two systems are meant to capture each employee's results and what he/she is hired for—things like their outputs, business results, successes, productivity, and other KPIs. Then, these results are rolled up to the group, department, and company levels. These technologies allow employees to log, track, and analyze their outputs, outcomes, results, revenues, and productivity across one employee, group of employees, or a job role. These technologies allow you to track, monitor, and measure TTP. Then, you can take the right action to shorten it if it is unacceptably long.

Some organizations track metrics like work efficiency, attendance, overall assessment scores, and quantitative metrics such as measuring the number of units produced.

Some organizations use software to measure the time employees take to complete a job based on signing in and signing out of each job. The system automatically calculates the difference in time to show that it took 3 hours to complete a job. The metric can then be aggregated or averaged and compared to those of other employees to see who is doing more work.

Leveraging analytics

But that data alone is not enough. You need powerful analytics to understand the trends at every level in the organization. A study published in the *International Journal of Management Science and Business Administration* found that using analytics to monitor employee performance can improve productivity and reduce costs.

Some examples are PowerBI and HANA; however, there are many more. These analytics are able to slice the data across several dimensions to figure out what really matters to the business or business unit and how they should matter in terms of employee proficiency. Based on that, proficiency metrics are defined.

As mentioned before, measuring the proficiency of positions like managers could be very difficult due to several unquantified and abstract or personal aspects of the job. Google's People Operations team has been using data analytics to measure employee proficiency and drive performance. For example, Google[23] developed Project Oxygen, which identified and measured the key behaviors of high-performing managers using a five-point scale through a survey of their employees. They used this baseline to improve managerial performance across the organization.

Some internal platforms, such as IBM, Accenture, PwC, Semiens, Salesforce, and Deloitte, are examples of how organizations leverage several pieces of employee data to assess overall proficiency. Such systems collect data from various sources, such as performance reviews, project assignments, and learning history, to analyze employee skills, areas, or improvements. By doing so, organizations have been reported to enhance employee proficiency and better align their workforce with their business objectives.

Assessment-driven proficiency measurement

Several organizations find it tedious and impractical to measure proficiency based on activities or even outcomes. They resort to using assessment-driven technologies and corresponding analytics. The idea is to measure employee skills and work out some sort of

---

[23]Garvin, D. A. (2013). How Google Sold Its Engineers on Management. Harvard Business Review. Retrieved from https://hbr.org/2013/12/how-google-sold-its-engineers-on-management

grading criteria. Skill proficiency is deemed an indication of the final proficiency expected from the role. This could be a false indicator at times because mastering a skill does not mean mastery of the overall job and the ability to produce the outcomes defined for the job. However, this is the easiest of all to work on this assumption. Thus, if you implement such technologies, keep in mind that any assessment, whether done by employees as self-assessment or done by supervisors, whether done during the training or done post-training, is not an accurate representation of an employee's proficiency in producing job outcomes.

Gamified homework and quizzes are a way to measure such proficiency, though the scope is limited in terms of the data that such assessments generate. For instance, Kahoot!, a Norwegian online game-based learning platform, builds gamified assessments; but remember that the goal of such technologies is to maintain engagement and challenge levels in self-learning mode. Modern LMSs, such as Talent LMS, support such games-based assessments. A more reasonable assessment mechanism is by using simulated assessments such as HackerRank or HackerEarth, where technical assessment is done during a live coding simulation.

TAKING IT FORWARD

In this chapter, you learned the second strategy and its considerations for implementing technologies to help organizations baseline and track proficiency thresholds for each job role. You read how these data are used to set the correct thresholds for each job role that employees must attain to be deemed as proficient. In the next chapter, you will learn the third strategy of the strategic leadership

5/ TECHNOLOGIES AND ANALYTICS FOR PROFICIENCY METRICS

framework to identify and measure the activities and work skills of employees.

Use the space below to reflect upon and note down your major takeaways to this point.

Reflections 5.1

Chapter 1
DIGITAL REVOLUTION IN LEARNING TECHNOLOGIES

Chapter 2
BUSINESS KPIs FOR LEARNING TECHNOLOGY

Chapter 3
STRATEGIC LEARNING TECHNOLOGY LEADERSHIP THINKING

Chapter 4
TECHNOLOGIES & ANALYTICS FOR HIRING RIGHT

Chapter 5
TECHNOLOGIES & ANALYTICS FOR PROFICIENCY METRICS

Chapter 6
TECHNOLOGIES & ANALYTICS FOR WORK SKILLS

Chapter 7
TECHNOLOGIES & ANALYTICS FOR EFFICIENT LEARNING PATH

Chapter 8
TECHNOLOGIES & ANALYTICS FOR TIME MEASUREMENTS

Chapter 9
EMERGING TECHNOLOGIES FOR SPEED

Chapter 10
THE FINAL THOUGHTS

BONUS
MODELLING GEN-AI FOR ENTERPRSE L&D

L&D CAREER RESOURCES

6

TECHNOLOGIES & ANALYTICS FOR WORK SKILLS

In the proficiency–time graph, the 'normal proficiency curve' length depends on how much you want new employees to learn and perform. That factor impacts how soon they will be there at that threshold proficiency.

If, instead of forcing your employees to learn everything, you give them smaller, pointed, just enough content or skills to master, they can come up-to speed to the desired proficiency thresholds in a shorter time.

WORK-SKILLS ANALYSIS

If you want to save time in employees' proficiency journey, you need to know where they are spending more time. To accomplish this, you have to have technologies and analytics to profile and analyze the following components of work and skills:

- At the first level, you need to analyze the work in terms of its nature, events, activities, tasks, and skills involved. You start with a documented understanding of work to understand what is involved in a given job or what employees are supposed to be doing to accomplish a task.
- At the next level, you track and analyze to deeply understand the activities or tasks that they are doing to produce the results. This may reveal several surprises.
- At the next level, you question whether everything done during a given task is relevant or necessary. Or, are they simply doing them to fulfill certain non-value-added obligations.

- Then, based on the observations, you can determine what is really important and what employees need to learn or perform in order to produce the business outcomes. This is what defines proficiency metrics. Perhaps some of the non-essential things can be eliminated or optimized (see next chapter also).

Fundamentally, you are determining the size, breadth, and extent of work skills (or context) that they need to master. You are figuring out what matters for training, learning, and job outcomes.

WORK-SKILLS ANALYTICS TECHNOLOGIES

The majority of the organizations that I had selected for my research study had highly advanced skill assessment data analytics. But, not all analytics helps with speed unless it is strategically designed for analyzing the skills and nature of activities to be performed by the employees. You need technology or analytics to help you to do two kinds of analysis.

1. *Activity (work) analytics*
2. *Skill analytics*

1. Work or activity analytics technologies

Activity or work analytics technologies help you assess:

- What is happening?
- How often is it/they are happening?

6/ TECHNOLOGIES AND ANALYTICS FOR WORK SKILLS

- What events are happening more often?
- What is anticipated but not happening?
- What are the high-impact tasks? Of these, what tasks are more complex?
- In what sequence are they happening?
- What needs to be done?
- What is the nature of activities to be performed by the employees?

Based on all these dimensions, you can define what really matters to produce the outcomes that are defined as part of the proficiency metrics. Your focus is to understand where people should spend most of their time and where they should not.

Data analytics on event frequency

Among the organizations I selected for my research study was a semiconductor equipment company. The company used tools like CRM and business intelligence (BI) to do robust work analyses on the work being performed. Their CRM system tracked the events and activities performed by the employees. They asked their employees for several years to log daily reports in terms of activities they performed on the machine, the time they spent, the materials they ordered/used, the root cause of the problem, and what resolution finally fixed the problem and things of that nature. They then plotted the aggregated data against different dimensions. It revealed a lot of intelligence that could be fed back into how to speed up employee proficiency.

One such revelation was from the Pareto of event frequencies. Among all the events that were happening over the years, only 30% were highly frequent, 20% were of mid-frequency, and the remaining 50% were of very low frequency.

However, when they look at their training and learning programs, they see that they were designed to train engineers for everything, just in case it happens. When you give employees too many things to master, irrespective of whether they encounter them, you are making the path much longer! And, if they don't encounter it often, they won't become proficient.

Taking that analytics intelligence, they redesigned the program. So, they redid their whole certification program. They created a sort of population pyramid. They trained all their engineers with programs that catered to the skills required to handle 30% of frequent events. Those events would happen so often that they would get a chance to master them. It naturally took less time to train and less time to become proficient. Their TTP was significantly reduced.

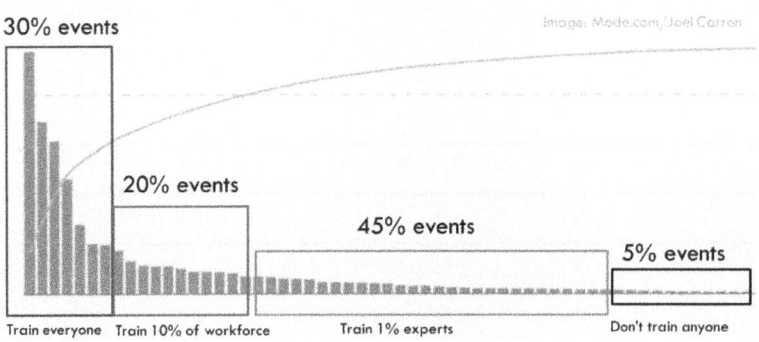

Figure 6.1: An example of using powerful activity analytics.

They then picked 10% of this population and trained them on specific skills required to handle the 20% mid-range frequency events. They were sort of go-to specialists, located in roughly one per country, who would handle such an event. For example, they were called upon when such events happened once every 3 months.

6/ TECHNOLOGIES AND ANALYTICS FOR WORK SKILLS

Since these smaller number of guys saw those mid-frequency events relatively more often, they also became proficient in those skills in shorter times.

Finally, they chose 1% of these specialists whose job was to fly around the world and handle 45% of very low-frequency events happening anywhere in the world. These events happened once in 2 years. They identified a handful of experts worldwide and continued flying to support those events. Since these guys supported only those events wherever they happened, they were exposed to them more often. Now, their workspace was so wide that they were definitely likely to see that event in some corner of the world. They got a chance to practice and become proficient in those low-frequency events.

Interestingly, they decided not to train anyone on the remaining 5% of events, which happened perhaps once in 5 years. They used PSSs instead that provide JIT, at the point of need info or skills—when you provide learners the knowledge at the point of application, it significantly speeds up proficiency.

By doing this, they massively shortened the TTP of engineers down to 50% in each group. The idea is not to make everyone an expert in everything. In fact, organizations don't need that many experts. If the larger population segment is proficient in most essential things, they will survive.

Business intelligence (BI) tools

BI tools are widely used to gather, analyze, and visualize employee performance and productivity data. It helps organizations to make data-driven decisions and improve their operations. For example, a company can use BI to analyze sales data and identify trends to improve its sales strategies.

Certain jobs involve the physical movement of employees. Internet of Things (IoT) connection allows for gathering data on employee behavior and performance. For example, sensors can be used to track how often employees use certain equipment or perform specific tasks.

2. Skill analytics technologies

Skill analytics technologies help you perform an advanced analysis of skills that employees have to use in order to support those activities, events, or solutions that matter the most. Once you have that information, you will understand what is important. In the next step (see next chapter), you can use this information to limit the number of skills or content to learn and master, which, in turn, shortens the time.

Such skill analysis also allows organizations to simply disposition tasks to PSSs, automation, and AI-based systems. The point is to understand the nature of work from analytics and then deploy the most efficient PSS that can cut short the need for massive upfront training. Rather offers JIT support.

AI-based skill analysis

As an example, Visier[24] used AI-based workforce analytics is used to analyze employee skills, identify skill gaps, and make data-driven decisions about training and development. JPMorgan Chase, an American multinational financial services firm, has been a pioneer in using employee analytics to identify skills gaps and upskilling

---

[24] Visier. Why Employee Skills Must Be Measured. https://www.visier.com/blog/why-employee-skills-must-be-measured/

needs[25]. By analyzing workforce data, the company is able to identify which skills were in high demand and which employees needed the training to develop those skills. This allows JPMorgan Chase to invest in targeted training programs and upskill its workforce, which improves employee retention and helps the company stay competitive.

TAKING IT FORWARD

In this chapter, you learned the third strategy and its considerations for implementing technologies to help organizations identify and analyze the work, the skills involved, and patterns of behaviors to accomplish outcomes. You understood how analytics needs to be applied strategically to ensure that you ask employees to master what is essential for the job. In the next chapter, you will learn the fourth strategy of the strategic leadership framework to design an efficient, lean, and optimal learning path for employees to attain desired proficiency thresholds in a shorter time.

Use the space below to reflect upon major takeaways.

---

[25] https://www.linkedin.com/pulse/workforce-analytics-journey-jp-morgan-chase-david-green

Reflections 6.1

Chapter 1
DIGITAL REVOLUTION IN LEARNING TECHNOLOGIES

Chapter 2
BUSINESS KPIs FOR LEARNING TECHNOLOGY

Chapter 3
STRATEGIC LEARNING TECHNOLOGY LEADERSHIP THINKING

Chapter 4
TECHNOLOGIES & ANALYTICS FOR HIRING RIGHT

Chapter 5
TECHNOLOGIES & ANALYTICS FOR PROFICIENCY METRICS

Chapter 6
TECHNOLOGIES & ANALYTICS FOR WORK SKILLS

Chapter 7
TECHNOLOGIES & ANALYTICS FOR EFFICIENT LEARNING PATH

Chapter 8
TECHNOLOGIES & ANALYTICS FOR TIME MEASUREMENTS

Chapter 9
EMERGING TECHNOLOGIES FOR SPEED

Chapter 10
THE FINAL THOUGHTS

BONUS
MODELLING GEN-AI FOR ENTERPRSE L&D

L&D CAREER RESOURCES

7

TECHNOLOGIES & ANALYTICS FOR EFFICIENT LEARNING PATH

7/ TECHNOLOGIES AND ANALYTICS FOR EFFICIENT LEARNING PATH

The fourth thing that you will notice on the proficiency–time graph is the angles that determine the lift up of the accelerated proficiency curve. This angle comes into the picture when you can design a highly efficient learning path that allows your employees to follow the accelerated proficiency curve.

The premise is simple—when employees are offered a lean, optimized, and laser-focused learning path, they need to learn only the most important content and skills, and, therefore, can progress faster. A substantial amount of time is cut out by avoiding wasteful activities that they don't need or have already mastered.

TECHNOLOGIES FOR EFFICIENT LEARNING PATHS

Once you understand what is required for a job role, you need to find parameters that can help you make that new path more efficient. For that, you need technologies and analytics to make the learning path adaptive and efficient.

These analytics will help you establish three things:

- First, analyze the sequences or learning paths your star players are following to achieve proficiency at an accelerated rate.
- Second, determine or establish the most optimized path across such star employees.
- Third, replicate the optimized path for the new hires.

The idea of this analytics is to manage the learning path of employees efficiently in a way that is designed for speed. The term 'learning path' represents employees' entire training and learning path until they attain the desired threshold of proficiency. Thus, this strategy pertains to the largest number of technologies, platforms, and tools.

Using technologies, you deliver the employee experiences in a very efficient and lean sequence to cut significant time. This has been conceptually shown in Figure 7.1.

Figure 7.1: Efficient and optimized proficiency path.

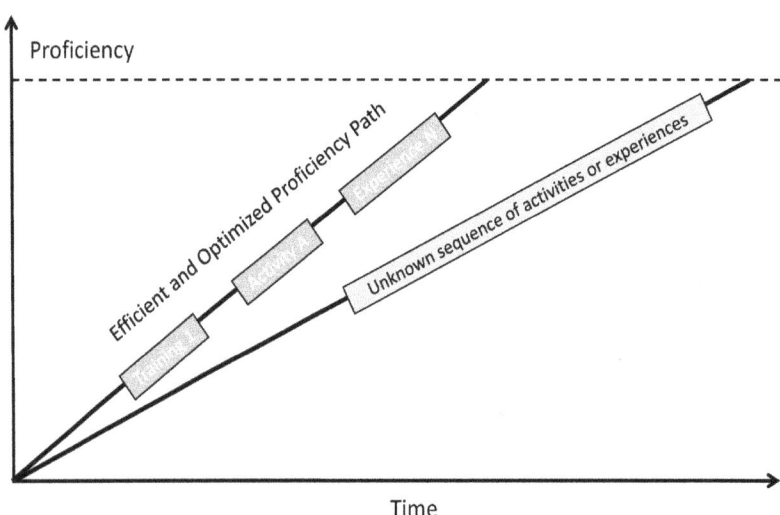

As part of the optimized sequence, your goal will be to provide learning and performance in the most time-efficient fashion. The primary focus of these technologies would be as follows:

- Redefine and optimize the sequence of required activities for a time-efficient path.
- Make each individual activity time-efficient by leveraging technologies.

- Eliminate non-essential activities from the path or replace certain activities with automation through technologies.
- Disposition of the time required for training to use job aids, PSSs, and workflow-based tools.

TECHNOLOGIES AND ANALYTICS

Until now, organizations have worked on various categories of technologies in isolation. The pandemic and the research on TTP have established that each category is not a self-sufficient solution. One has to integrate various technologies throughout the learning path to impact employee TTP.

You should know an important point before diving into the categories of such technologies. Merely using these technologies, gadgets, or analytics to do some tasks or activities would not shorten or optimize the learning path. You need to deliberately insert activities that force employees to use these technologies in lieu of other resources or activities like training. With these technologies, you must be able to replace some time-consuming, lengthy, inefficient, irrelevant, or not-so-essential activities. Only then will you be able to achieve an efficient, optimized, and lean learning path that allows a much shorter TTP.

Here are a few major categories, and this list is evolving.

Algorithmic LMS

Some organizations use algorithmic LMS, which will adjust the learning path and make it adaptive based on the prior skills of the learners and how well they are doing. The assignments, hurdles, and learning modules adapt automatically based on ratings, results, and progression. It could also recommend assignments, projects, or focus areas for learners to complete in a certain sequence faster than before.

PSSs

The most powerful technologies are PSSs. Many tasks don't need to be learned upfront because one can seek help in the form of tools or aid or a system like decision-support software when needed. When people learn and apply in their time of need, their time to mastery is shortened. Chapter 8 details eight types of emerging PSSs and how they all help to shorten TTP.

AR-based technologies

You could add certain tasks or assignments which can be mastered with AR and VR technologies. These are the latest in the breed technologies. The advantage of such technologies is that they provide workflow-based training that is made available instantly at the time of need. Some of those, like AR HoloLens, support having a network of coaches from different locations to watch employees and guide them remotely in real time. VR technologies are one notch up in terms of providing a highly immersive experience in jobs like military combat, firefighting, and medical, allowing them to accumulate near-life experience faster. Chapter 8 details some use cases of these technologies under learning technologies and PSSs.

Immersive gaming environments

You could add simulated experience into the learning path if such a real experience is not possible in the real world. Some companies are using full-scale immersive gaming environments like underground mines to teach the dangers of fire underground, which otherwise may take years to master. Chapter 10 highlights some use cases of these technologies under learning technologies.

7/ TECHNOLOGIES AND ANALYTICS FOR EFFICIENT LEARNING PATH

Virtual training and social connectivity tools

On-demand self-guided training can optimize the learning path as learners don't have to wait for an instructor-led event. Additionally, virtual training technologies allow you to quickly scale up instructor-led training capacity if employees are waiting for such an event for a significant time. Increasing capacity may have an indirect impact on the time-to-readiness. Deliberately inserting such learning avenues into the learning path certainly can make it more efficient. On top of that, you can replace certain tasks with collaborative work via social tools, which can allow new employees to quickly and informally connect with star players, cutting a considerable amount of time out of the equation. Chapter 8 details some use cases of these technologies under learning technologies and PSSs.

ADAPTIVE LEARNING PATH

Among all, adaptive learning technologies are finding more and more ground. Some organizations use analytics that are quite established and continuously update the learning profile of learners.

Personalized adaptive learning paths technologies

One of the crucial aspects of employee training is ensuring that the learning paths are optimized for everyone's needs and skill levels. Learning experience platforms are focused on providing employees with personalized, interactive learning experiences. They use ML algorithms to recommend the content to learners based on their interests, learning goals, and job responsibilities. By leveraging these technologies, organizations can create personalized, engaging, and effective learning experiences that help employees acquire new skills and knowledge more efficiently, shorten the learning curve, and improve their performance on the job.

AI can capture, aggregate, and analyze data from several different sources to build a student learning profile. AI-based learning systems can provide trainers with useful information about students' learning styles, abilities, and progress and provide personalized learning experiences based on this data.

AI-based systems can conduct pre-assessments to evaluate students' existing knowledge and identify the areas of strengths and weaknesses. The system can then suggest a learning path and specific content based on the pre-assessment, which can improve learning effectiveness. Some AI or algorithmic LMS systems can determine if the next set of modules, tasks, skills, or content is applicable based on their prior achievements. The subsequent learning path is adjusted or adapted dynamically.

Some organizations leveraged various analytics and tools to determine the most optimum sequence of activities, such as training modules, on-the-job assignments, and projects, to keep learners focused on what drives their proficiency toward the target. Such technologies match the profile of each and every learner to resources that are appropriate for them, thereby improving learning outcomes. By gathering data on an employee's skill level and preferred learning style, analytics can be used to deliver personalized training content that is tailored to his/her specific needs. This can help ensure that employees are engaged in the learning process and that they are able to learn more effectively.

This technology can measure the progress and effectiveness of the learning path and provide valuable insights to both students and teachers. This can optimize and personalize the learning experience for students and help teachers grade more quickly and accurately. AI-

7/ TECHNOLOGIES AND ANALYTICS FOR EFFICIENT LEARNING PATH

based adaptive learning systems can adjust the content, pace, and sequence of learning based on the student's performance and understanding. The technology can provide personalized feedback and offer learning recommendations to enhance the student's understanding and mastery of the subject. Analytics can be used to gather data on employee performance and identify areas where additional training may be necessary. For example, analytics can be used to track employee progress through a training program and identify areas where they may be struggling or where additional resources may be needed to help them succeed.

This path is also modified based on the trainer, mentor, or manager's ratings. It could also recommend assignments, projects, or focus areas for learners to complete in a certain sequence faster. The learning profile is updated as and when they complete any assignment, module, project, rated by mentors, or other achievements during their learning and work.

Some examples of such adaptive systems are Wiley's Knewton, DreamBox, and Area9 Rhapsode.

Adaptive mentoring technologies

One organization used a profiling tool to identify who the right mentors were. Normally, mentors are paired like "Go sit with Joe, and if Joe is not available, sit with Jim." Or better organizations pair them based on skills and competencies or functional areas. What if the organization could pair them based on goals for speed? If selected carefully and matched carefully, such people can mentor new employees, induct the correct success behaviors, and give them the best sequence to learn the skills that can cut short a huge amount of time from the path.

Overall, using analytics in employee training and development can help optimize individual employees' learning paths, improve learning outcomes, and ultimately lead to a more skilled and productive workforce.

TAKING IT FORWARD

In this chapter, you learned the fourth strategy and its considerations for implementing technologies to help organizations design an efficient, lean, and optimal learning path for employees to attain desired proficiency thresholds in a shorter time. You developed an understanding of how algorithmic and adaptive technologies will allow you to create accelerated learning paths. In the next chapter, you will learn the fifth and the last strategy of the strategic leadership framework to implement technologies to measure time, including activity time and TTP.

Use the space below to reflect upon and note down your major takeaways to this point.

7/ TECHNOLOGIES AND ANALYTICS FOR EFFICIENT LEARNING PATH

Reflections 7.1

Chapter 1
DIGITAL REVOLUTION IN LEARNING TECHNOLOGIES

Chapter 2
BUSINESS KPIs FOR LEARNING TECHNOLOGY

Chapter 3
STRATEGIC LEARNING TECHNOLOGY LEADERSHIP THINKING

Chapter 4
TECHNOLOGIES & ANALYTICS FOR HIRING RIGHT

Chapter 5
TECHNOLOGIES & ANALYTICS FOR PROFICIENCY METRICS

Chapter 6
TECHNOLOGIES & ANALYTICS FOR WORK SKILLS

Chapter 7
TECHNOLOGIES & ANALYTICS FOR EFFICIENT LEARNING PATH

Chapter 8
TECHNOLOGIES & ANALYTICS FOR TIME MEASUREMENTS

Chapter 9
EMERGING TECHNOLOGIES FOR SPEED

Chapter 10
THE FINAL THOUGHTS

BONUS
MODELLING GEN-AI FOR ENTERPRSE L&D

L&D CAREER RESOURCES

8

TECHNOLOGIES & ANALYTICS FOR TIME MEASUREMENTS

8/ TECHNOLOGIES AND ANALYTICS FOR TIME MEASUREMENTS

The most common sense but ignored strategy is measuring the time throughout the journey. Unless you measure the time, how can you expect to reduce it or accelerate it in the first place? You need to know precisely when employees are reaching the desired proficiency metrics in a job role. So, you need technologies to track time at every stage of an employee's learning path. How long was it taking before, and how much is it taking now? How much time have they spent already? How much time can be shortened? You need this information at the individual and group levels.

For that, you need technologies and analytics that help you track and analyze time variables.

TIME-TO-ACTIVITY VS TTP

Let me first explain the traditional approach to measuring time spent on activities or time of task completion. I will then highlight why such an approach has flaws and what you, as a learning technologist, can do about it.

Measuring time-on-activities

Basic systems like LMS, CRM, and ERM all have time stamps. These days, several organizations are using specialized time-tracking apps and analytics tools, both implicitly and explicitly. Most of these are meant to directly measure the time spent on activities, tasks, projects, or jobs and then analyze the patterns to optimize workforce management.

Here are some examples:

Employee monitoring software

These software are designed to track an employee's activity on their work computer. They collect, store, and analyze data about the websites visited, search queries, applications used, and external storage devices used during the workday. For instance, Teramind[26] tracks employee work, engagement levels, and activities. It also provides real-time alerts on suspicious behavior, such as data breaches and insider threats.

Time-tracking tools

These tools allow employees to track the time spent on each task, project, or activity. Some popular time-tracking tools are Clockify, Toggl, and RescueTime. For instance, Clockify[27] provides detailed reports on how much time was spent on each task and project, which can be used for billing, payroll, and productivity analysis.

Performance management software

These software help employers to set goals, track progress, and provide feedback to employees. They can also be used to measure the time spent on each task or project. Examples of performance management software include BambooHR, ClearCompany, and Cornerstone OnDemand. For instance, Microsoft[28] Workplace Analytics provides insights into communication patterns and other employee work habits. It tracks email and calendar metadata, which can be used to understand how employees spend their time and collaborate with others.

---

[26] https://www.teramind.co/
[27] https://clockify.me/
[28] https://www.intlock.com/blog/microsoft-workplace-analytics/

8/ TECHNOLOGIES AND ANALYTICS FOR TIME MEASUREMENTS

Project management tools

These tools help teams to collaborate and manage projects. They often include time-tracking features that allow employees to log time spent on each task or project. Examples of project management tools include Asana, Basecamp, and Trello.

HR analytics dashboards

These customizable dashboards organize KPIs and other visualizations in meaningful and engaging ways for decision-makers. They can be used to track employee turnover rates, time-to-fill positions, and other important HR metrics.

But here is the problem—most of them capture only things like the time taken to finish an activity, project, or job. Is that enough? Let us see the issue below.

Measuring TTP

Let us take one example, as shown in Figure 8.1. At an organization, the proficiency measures they chose for salespeople is when the time to close a sale is less than 10 days, consistent over 2 months. This means that the time-to-closure is measured in each sale. An individual may sell 100 things in a month, but the key parameter is if the sales cycle is 10 days or fewer each time.

A group of salespeople delivered a time-to-closure of 25 days, 15 days, 10 days, and so forth each month.

As you see, the group hit 10-day sales cycle in month 3 but then went down again. The first time they showed that proficiency was at the end of 6 months because they were consistent for 2 months.

Most analytics and technologies can only capture time to sales closure. But here, TTP is 6 months. You can't measure it unless technologies are made to measure it.

Figure 8.1: Measuring time-to-activity versus TTP

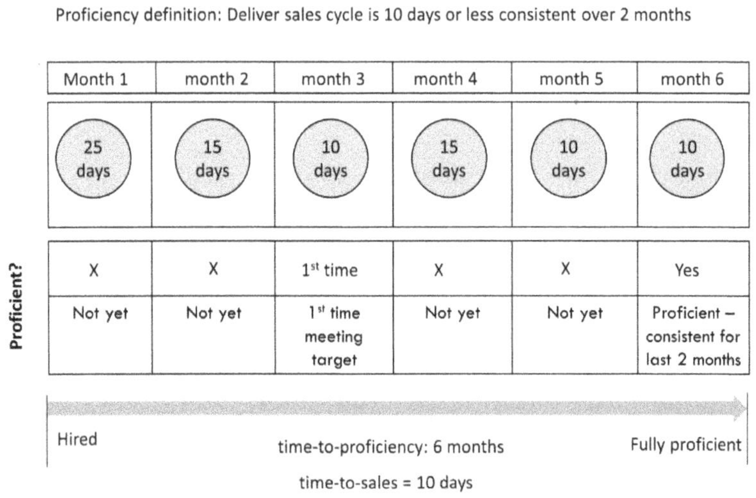

Proficiency definition: Deliver sales cycle is 10 days or less consistent over 2 months

	Month 1	month 2	month 3	month 4	month 5	month 6
	25 days	15 days	10 days	15 days	10 days	10 days
Proficient?	X	X	1st time	X	X	Yes
	Not yet	Not yet	1st time meeting target	Not yet	Not yet	Proficient – consistent for last 2 months

Hired → time-to-proficiency: 6 months → Fully proficient
time-to-sales = 10 days

Things go wrong when organizations take that data on time-to-closure and try to squeeze it down without even knowing if their sales force is already proficient enough to deliver the current time-to-closure numbers or not. Tracking such KPIs does not help in shortening TTPs in any way. Rather, it creates a mad rush!

We simply waste the capabilities of our technologies in measuring the time required for the activity.

8/ TECHNOLOGIES AND ANALYTICS FOR TIME MEASUREMENTS

STRATEGIC STANCE ON TIME MEASUREMENT

The nuisance of using time-stamped activity data

Here is an ironic observation across the industry. Most organizations set very aggressive time targets for their staff's actions. They continue measuring to see if employees delivered as per agreed timelines or not, regardless of how realistic or practical those timelines are.

In this process, they rarely measure the total time taken to perform an activity, except in production settings where time comes as a commodity.

They don't do much historical analysis on trends in how people have become time-efficient in mastering things within that assigned time. The key issue is that such analytics to track time to mastery across seasoned employees typically do not exist.

The closest you can achieve is using the timestamps that data collection systems provide. Much processing and analysis are required to aggregate it at the job and task levels and establish an actual time to mastery or ascertain TTP. However, such data are typically poorly integrated since most technologies and analytics are procured at the departmental level for individual functions. Thus, drawing TTP measurements from time-stamped activity data can be a computational nightmare.

Lack of technologies and analytics for TTP measurements

At the time of writing this book, there were no specific technologies mentioned that leading organizations use to track and measure TTP metrics of employees. Straightforward, off-the-shelf, or even customizable analytics did not currently exist in the market. In my research, I observed that most organizations don't have suitable measurement mechanisms for TTP or reporting mechanisms on their dashboards. The lack of these systems is the fundamental reason why focus on shortening TTP does not even arise.

Way around for the time being

However, organizations can use various metrics and practices to track employee productivity and measure the time it takes for employees to achieve a specified level of proficiency.

One of the ways to track TTP is by using the metric of 'time-to-productivity.' This metric assesses how long it takes an employee to achieve a specified level of proficiency and can be useful when onboarding new employees who have to learn a new skill or set of skills. Organizations can also use the average time employees take to reach proficiency to calculate the cost of making a new employee proficient.

One of the organizations involved in my research study used time-to-productivity in terms of business outcomes, such as the number of machine parts finished. Their tracking system showed an exponential curve of how productivity improved over time and when it first and then when it consistently met the set criteria. Usually, such quantifiable measures are great.

Another organization involved in my research study used 'time-to-certification' as a measure of proficiency. But using it has some shortfalls. If the definition of being certified simply means initial readiness for the job and not full proficiency, then it is impossible to use 'time-to-certification' as a measure.

8/ TECHNOLOGIES AND ANALYTICS FOR TIME MEASUREMENTS

Usually, such quantifiable measures are great. But how would you measure the TTP of a manager? The TTP of such job roles would be challenging to track, especially when such professionals are simply thrown into the fire.

Strategic focus on TTP measurements

To measure time, you have to have a strategic focus. But on top of that, you must have sound systems or infrastructure to find the time for proficiency data. One single technology may not be enough. You may have to synchronize several analytics tools and dashboards to build an organization-wide TTP dashboard. As a learning technologist, you must determine the collection of technologies and analytics to track, baseline, and monitor TTP.

Ideally, you would want to track TTP at the individual level, then roll it up to the group level, followed by job role level, departmental level, and so on. Thus, technologies need to support measuring TTP at multiple levels within an organization.

That becomes our baseline. And then, we have to set specific targets for how much we want to bring it down. For instance, is a salesperson becoming fully proficient in 6 months acceptable? If not, what is an acceptable number? That discussion determines how much TTP should be shortened by technologies.

The final improvement targets need to be tracked by technologies over time. You must put together monthly or quarterly dashboards to show improvements and challenges at the group, departmental, and organizational levels. At the same time, you have to have a mechanism to do competitive benchmarking with your peers to see if you are indeed developing your employees faster enough.

TAKING IT FORWARD

In this chapter, you learned the last strategy of the strategic leadership framework to implement technologies to measure time, including activity duration and TTP. You learned that despite time being a common sense measurement, it is the hardest to measure because none of the technologies support such a measurement directly.

Use the space below to reflect upon and note down your major takeaways to this point.

In the next chapter, you will go through some of the emerging trends in learning technologies, workplace analytics, PSSs, social technologies, and AI-based technologies, which all have great potential to speed up employee development.

8/ TECHNOLOGIES AND ANALYTICS FOR TIME MEASUREMENTS

Reflections 8.1

Chapter 1
DIGITAL REVOLUTION IN LEARNING TECHNOLOGIES

Chapter 2
BUSINESS KPIs FOR LEARNING TECHNOLOGY

Chapter 3
STRATEGIC LEARNING TECHNOLOGY LEADERSHIP THINKING

Chapter 4
TECHNOLOGIES & ANALYTICS FOR HIRING RIGHT

Chapter 5
TECHNOLOGIES & ANALYTICS FOR PROFICIENCY METRICS

Chapter 6
TECHNOLOGIES & ANALYTICS FOR WORK SKILLS

Chapter 7
TECHNOLOGIES & ANALYTICS FOR EFFICIENT LEARNING PATH

Chapter 8
TECHNOLOGIES & ANALYTICS FOR TIME MEASUREMENTS

Chapter 9
EMERGING TECHNOLOGIES FOR SPEED

Chapter 10
THE FINAL THOUGHTS

BONUS
MODELLING GEN-AI FOR ENTERPRSE L&D

L&D CAREER RESOURCES

9
EMERGING TECHNOLOGIES FOR SPEED

9/ EMERGING TECHNOLOGIES FOR SPEED

I conducted a massive study with over 70 world-class organizations with success stories to have shortened the TTP of their employees. I found that several organizations used technology as one of the key mechanisms to shorten TTP. The technologies used by organizations varied from one context to the other. For instance, organizations in cutting-edge financial services used state-of-the-art technologies, while those in retail businesses used more accessible technologies. Based on the end goal, I saw that these technologies fall into five groups.

1. **Workplace Analytics:** The first group is related to technologies that are primarily meant for workforce analytics. Those included technologies to track talent metrics, performance metrics, activity metrics, and skill metrics.
2. **Learning Technologies:** The second group is related to learning, teaching, and training technologies. These include activities such as designing and delivering training, distributing, and accessing content, certification, and assessments.
3. **Performance Support Technologies:** The third group is related to technologies that support the performance of employees in the field or on the job. These include mentoring or coaching tools, job aids, resources, procedures, tools, and automation.
4. **Social Technologies:** The fourth group involves those technologies that support social connections, networks, communities, and interactions.
5. **AI-based technologies:** The last group of technologies is AI-based technologies, which are still evolving and have been blowing the organizational and technological thinking process across the Internet.

Figure 9.1: Emerging technologies for speed.

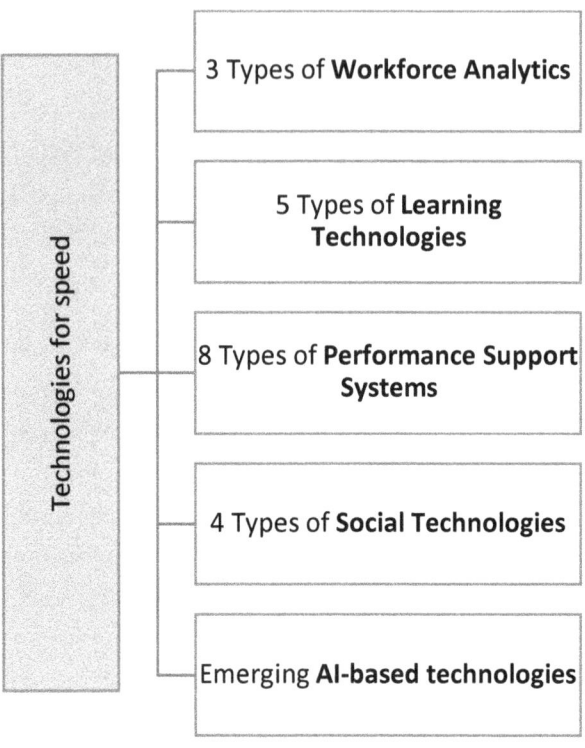

Businesses are changing at a high speed. Is your technology strategy enabling you to prepare employees for what's coming?

THREE TYPES OF WORKFORCE ANALYTICS

Analytics have been detailed in previous chapters. This section aims to provide an overall spectrum of analytics.

9/ EMERGING TECHNOLOGIES FOR SPEED

The analytics spectrum

In the market, there are several similar-sounding terms like people analytics, talent analytics, human capital analytics, HR analytics, workforce analytics, and then finally, learning analytics. However, many of these terms may have overlapping meanings. The names are often adopted by the supplier or vendor, even if the intent of the analytics is similar to other analytics. However, one common thing is that all of these involve the use of data analytics to better understand and manage human resources in organizations.

While these terms may have some overlap in meaning, there are also important differences between them. People analytics and human capital analytics are broad terms encompassing multiple areas of HR management, while talent analytics, HR analytics, and workforce analytics focus on more specific areas of HR management. Learning analytics is a distinct area that focuses on improving learning and development programs.

People analytics is a term that broadly encompasses the use of data analytics to improve human resource management in organizations. It includes the analysis of data related to people processes, functions, challenges, and opportunities at work to achieve sustainable business success. People analytics focuses on providing meaningful insights into various types of HR data to contribute to the business's bottom line.

Talent analytics refers specifically to the use of data analytics to manage talent within an organization, including talent acquisition, development, retention, and succession planning.

Human capital analytics is a broader term that includes analyzing all human capital-related data in an organization, including financial and non-financial metrics. It is used to gain insights into how human capital investments are impacting business outcomes.

Figure 9.2: Various terms for workplace analytics.

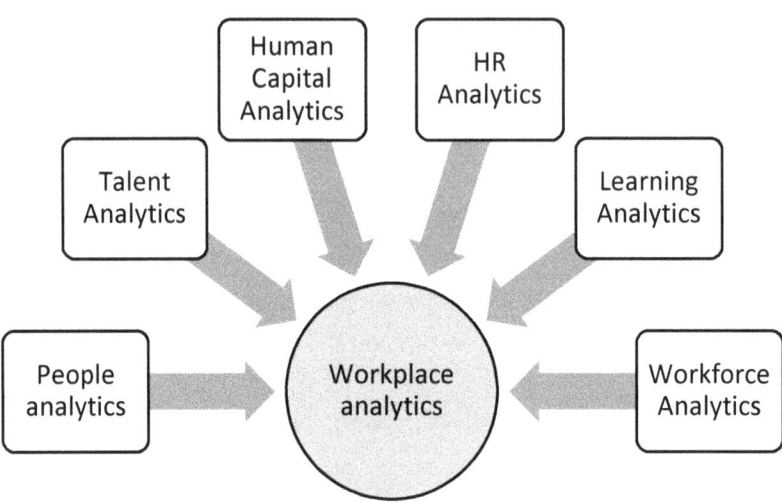

HR analytics uses data analytics to measure the impact of HR metrics, such as time to hire and retention rate, on business performance. HR analytics is a people-oriented function that aims to enable management and HR teams to make strategic and data-driven workforce decisions to improve workplace issues.

Workforce analytics focuses on assessing and using tools to drive decisions related to workforce management. It involves analyzing data on workforce productivity, hiring, performance management, compensation, and retention.

Learning analytics involves using data analytics to analyze and improve learning and development programs within an organization.

9/ EMERGING TECHNOLOGIES FOR SPEED

It includes measuring the effectiveness of training programs and identifying areas for improvement.

Despite the differences among these terms, it sometimes becomes hard to draw boundaries. But here is the good news! Technologies are converging. So, the lines between these analytics are now blurry. We call the collection of these analytics 'workplace analytics.' This includes the characteristics of the people as well as the characteristics of the work they do.

Analytics in the context of employee proficiency journey

It may become even more difficult for you to fully control all the analytics as a leader. Thus, your ability to take up a massive project of integrating diverse, incompatible analytics might be limited. Instead, I recommend looking at analytics in the context of the employee proficiency journey.

The hiring stage

Whether internal or external, some organizations have analytics that deal with talent distribution, experience profiles, recruitment sources, and time to hire. Some examples of data captured at this stage are:

- Education profiles
- Diversity distribution
- Age distribution
- Talent profiles
- Retention metrics
- Time to hire trends
- Compensation comparisons

- Skill/experience analytics
- Service time
- Average experience
- Education
- Service time
- Project experience
- Past achievements
- Past role history
- Diversity eligibility
- Potential ratings
- Past performance ratings
- Talent profiles
- Skill assessments

The onboarding and orientation stage

We have some analytics on completing mandatory web-based training or other compliance training data via LMS. Some examples of data captured at this stage are:

- Dropout rate
- Time to orientation
- Manager's ratings
- First 90-days performance
- Compliance training records
- 90-days skill assessments

The training or coaching stage

We have some learning analytics that show us the training modules taken, skill profiles, skill gaps, and assessments from coaches. Some examples of data captured at this stage are:

9/ EMERGING TECHNOLOGIES FOR SPEED

- Training records
- Time in training
- Performance in training
- Trainer's scores
- Assessment scores
- Manager's ratings
- Compliance scores
- Mentor ratings
- Training costs

The on-the-job support stage

Only some analytics analyze the case activities, events, and performance of field folks. Some examples of data captured at this stage are:

- OJT records
- Mentor ratings
- Time to certification
- Field performance
- Skill assessment scores
- Manager's ratings
- Performance ratings
- Engagement metrics

The proficiency stage

We have some analytics that measure business KPIs across departments, regions, or even at the employee level. Some examples of data captured at this stage are:

- Customer satisfaction scores

- Customer calls
- Revenue generated
- Sales closures
- Case resolutions
- Time to resolution
- Financials & expenses

Strategic thinking for Implementing analytics

Here is the problem. The most commonly found workplace analytics are categorized as functional since each of them serves a specific purpose or goal for a department. At each phase of the employee development journey, the analytics used have some specific purpose within its intended function in business operations. While these analytics play an important role in each functional unit, there is no clear-cut anchor on how these analytics enable the speed of employee development.

The learning technology department does not own all analytics. Business units may own some, and the HR department may own others. For instance, learning analytics may include metrics on time to certification, and workforce analytics may have analytics on measuring time-to-productivity in the field.

Due to those silos, no analytics can measure speed as a universal metric across an organization. These functional boundaries also don't give us a common anchor to measure and increase the speed of employee development. If you can't tie off different analytics, you will have difficulty building a collective picture to understand whether we are going slow or fast. Hence, the decision on strategies to speed up

9/ EMERGING TECHNOLOGIES FOR SPEED

employee development becomes more qualitative in nature than based on data.

Employee performance cannot be accelerated unless that acceleration is measured and the time is quantifiably cut out of the equation. Therefore, the strategic questions that you need to focus on are: How do we integrate different workplace analytics to help in bringing employees up-to speed quickly? How do we rope them together so that it tells us a single high-level picture?

One way is to look at three categories of work analytics, irrespective of which functional department owns it:

1) Analytics for performer profiling (see Chapter 5)

2) Analytics for proficiency metrics (see Chapter 6)

3) Analytics for work skills (see Chapter 7)

The application of these analytics in the context of five strategies has already been explained in previous chapters.

FIVE TYPES OF LEARNING TECHNOLOGIES

The next set of technologies that impact speed are related to training and learning. Perhaps the name 'learning techs' is not that intuitive anymore because now the boundary between learning and work is diffused. Most of the learning technologies can make learning accessible, flexible, cost-effective, and more scalable, among other benefits. But only a few of them really have the potential to impact the speed-to-proficiency. In order to influence TTP, learning technologies must cut the time out of the employee development journey.

I observed five kinds of learning technologies in my research that showed good potential and success stories for shortening TTP.

1. *Adaptive LMS*
2. *Training delivery technologies*
3. *On-demand and mobile learning technologies*
4. *AR/VR learning technologies*
5. *Immersive and gamification technologies*

1. Adaptive LMS

The first group of technologies is those related to LMSs. LMSs typically are comparable across the board and do not directly impact the speed of employee development. Two kinds of LMSs that hold the potential to impact TTP are 1) The ones that support on-demand online learning and 2) The others that support adaptive learning paths. The adaptive paths are explained in detail in Chapter 6. In a nutshell, adaptive paths can enable differently skilled people to complete learning requirements via different routes if the system determines them qualified. That shortens times for certain employees.

Several LMSs provide adaptive learning paths, including Absorb LMS, Cornerstone, iSpring Learn, TalentLMS, Moodle, Litmos, Canvas LMS, Blackboard Learn, and Google Classroom. These systems use algorithms to optimize the learner's learning experience, resulting in better retention of new information and a more personalized learning experience. Some of these systems use ML-based adaptive systems, while others use an advanced algorithm, rules-based, or decision-tree adaptive systems. Cornerstone is an AI-powered system that helps accomplish this adaptive function of optimizing the content presented to learners based on their goals and current state of knowledge. This personalized learning experience can help learners better retain new information.

2. Training delivery technologies

The second technology group is related to training or delivering learning, content, skills, or classroom experiences.

Virtual training delivery technologies

During the pandemic, you have seen vast applications of virtual or remote training technologies. Now, the world is moving to virtual learning platforms, which allows for the quick addition of much capacity to run many people through programs. If people wait for instructor-led training to get started for their jobs, then adding capacity via virtual mode can help shorten the curve.

Keep in mind that while training delivery technologies make learning more accessible, they may also hinder the speed of employee development. For instance, in a social interaction-intensive job role, when you try to put the employees through an endless stream of online learning, you will see that their speed gets impacted negatively.

The reason is that most of the technologies in the learning space still tend to be largely content-focused. Thus, when choosing learning technology, focus on skills, not content.

Teaching technologies also include those used to conduct skill assessments, tools, and resources for coaching and mentoring.

Assessment technologies

Among them, the technologies that allow conducting multi-level assessments of employees can significantly increase employee speed. However, remember that the assessment only adds to speed if integrated into LMS or workforce analytics.

Mentoring and coaching technologies

Experiencing the job under someone qualified allows much faster proficiency than learning the same task in the classroom. However, organizations are often too focused on implementing formal training technologies, and they don't invest enough in technologies that could enable efficient coaching and mentoring processes.

The technologies that support distributed coaching and mentoring access to anyone, anywhere, and at any time hold the highest potential to accelerate proficiency. If employees are geographically dispersed or mostly work in the field, then your organizations must invest in 'on-the-go' coaching platforms that provide learners the required coaching when needed. Such platforms also equip experts with tools, templates, tracking, and other mechanisms to coach employees efficiently.

3. On-demand and mobile learning technologies

When employees get just enough information at the time of need, during the workflow, their speed of learning is seen to improve. The third group is mobile learning and self-paced learning technologies, which allow JIT learning. These are used to enable employees to learn on the go. It can speed up the process of acquiring and accessing the learning content faster when and where they need it.

9/ EMERGING TECHNOLOGIES FOR SPEED

Mobile learning

Mobile learning technologies offer a range of options to speed up learning, from gamification and microlearning apps to VR and personalized learning paths. Employing a combination of these technologies can help learners engage with and retain information more effectively.

However, remember that mobile learning must be integrated into on-demand, JIT PSSs to make a dent in learning speed. Such PSSs deliver learning as short modules or microlearning chunks over a period of time (check the next section about performance support technologies).

Mobile apps accessible on users' smartphones provide a convenient and accessible way to learn on the go. These can offer a range of content, including videos and interactive videos, that enhance learning outcomes. Microlearning apps such as Your Primer offer short courses in various disciplines. These apps allow learners to learn on the go and in short bursts, increasing retention and application of knowledge.

Quizzes and simulations

Mobile learning also includes quizzes and simulations to encourage continuous practice and hone previously learned skills. These mobile learning examples can include a range of formats, including multiple-choice, true or false, and drag-and-drop, among others.

4. AR/VR learning technologies

The augmented technologies are basically now on the storm. AR and VR technologies are revolutionizing the education industry by providing students with immersive experiences that enhance learning outcomes. Check out the next section on PSSs as well.

In cases where it is necessary to explore specific equipment and learn how to use it, an AR application can present the required 3D model and helpful explanations. This adds practical value to traditional learning materials and increases student engagement.

Smart glasses

A simpler version is augmented smart glasses, in which the screen is made available on the headset as a teaching aid. For instance, RealWear[29] and Google SmartGlases (launched a few years ago, now discontinued) offer displays on the glasses whereby employees can play step-by-step instructions or videos on these augmented displays while learning to do the task with their hands.

AR headsets

AR technology overlays digital information onto the real world via an augmented or heads-up display, enhancing the user's experience. AR can be used for gaming, education, and marketing. Among the latest technologies, Microsoft Hololens[30] and Oculus Quest[31] have an augmented display in front of your eyes on which employees can run immersive models, videos, instructions, procedures, or other learning material while doing a task with their hands. On that list, Apple's VisionPro has pushed the boundaries to integrate the real and virtual worlds. For example, repairing a machine needs both hands. Many of you have experienced or seen it in some videos. They can control it

---

[29]https://www.realwear.com/field-services/
[30]https://www.microsoft.com/en-us/hololens/hardware
[31]https://www.meta.com/quest/products/quest-2/

9/ EMERGING TECHNOLOGIES FOR SPEED

with voice commands or gestures, learn a step, and perform that step or check back instructions to do it again.

AR handheld devices and apps

Handheld AR is using handheld devices such as smartphones or tablets on which AR apps are installed to access and apply AR. These are easy to use and cheap. An example of a smartphone-based app is ScopeAR[32] which runs an AR model to repair and maintain the equipment with the help of remote experts. Another example is the Medical Realities[33] App, which uses AR and VR for medical training using gamified learning. Trainees can view medical procedures and lessons, full medical procedure simulations, instructions, and videos using Oculus and other AR devices. Such AR or VR devices are used in hospitals in real-life scenarios and medical colleges for the assessment and delivery of training in medical courses.

VR gadgets

The next extension is VR, which puts you close to the real virtual world. A fully digital environment that surrounds the user and makes them feel like they are in a real place. VR can be used for various purposes, such as gaming, education, and training.

Some tasks may not be practical or may be risky to do in the actual environment. For example, practicing putting out a fire, handling medical emergencies, or even combat situations in war. Those can be effectively taught using VR.

Some other examples are where a more immersive experience is needed. For instance, Mondly VR[34], a language learning platform,

---

[32] https://www.scopear.com/
[33] https://www.medicalrealities.com/technology
[34] https://www.mondly.com/vr

enables students to have real conversations with real people in VR, enhancing their language skills and making learning more engaging and effective.

VR can break the boundaries of experiences. For instance, Nearpod VR[35] offers virtual field trips to places that are otherwise inaccessible or harmful, such as ancient Egypt or the bottom of the ocean. This technology appeals to visual learners and provides engaging, real-life experiences.

The above examples demonstrate the vast potential of AR and VR technologies in enhancing and speeding up the learning experience. It is seen that several corporations will be able to shorten their TTP in the long run when they use AR and VR as part of the training delivery.

5. Immersive technologies, gamification and mixed Reality

Immersive technology refers to a class of tools that create immersive experiences with digital elements that feel real to the user, while gamification is a technique used to engage users and increase their participation by adding game-like features to non-game contexts.

Virtual world on computers

Combining these two elements allows designers to build a gamified virtual world on computers. These gaming scenarios give employees a sensory experience and feedback while solving realistic situations. For instance, an underground mining company built an entire underground mine virtually to train their employees to tackle the different hazardous conditions that they are likely to face. Obviously,

---

[35]https://nearpod.com/nearpod-vr

9/ EMERGING TECHNOLOGIES FOR SPEED

you would not want to train them in the actual event. But prepare them through immersive technologies to handle those challenging and hazardous situations.

Gamification

A simple example of gamification is the Yousician[36] music learning app that uses gamification to motivate users to practice by providing instant feedback, rewarding progress, and allowing users to compete with friends.

Among other examples of creating gamification are interactive leaderboards used in businesses to encourage employees to improve by making them aware that the rest of the team can see their progress.

On those lines, Salesforce's Trailhead gamified the onboarding process for employees, where users earn badges and points for completing training modules.

Some platforms are now able to use microlearning with gamification, which involves learning in short bursts, with gamification elements that engage users and increase their participation.

AR, VR, and MR gamification

Currently, there are more advanced methods, like AR and VR, used separately to create gamification, which is far more real and far more immersive than experiencing it on a computer. In some examples, AR and VR technologies could create immersive learning experiences that simulate real-life scenarios, like enabling students to explore far-

---

[36]https://yousician.com/lp/yousician

off lands or dive deep beneath the ocean surface without leaving the classroom.

Technological advances have evolved mixed reality, combining VR and AR elements to create a more immersive experience. MR can be used for gaming, education, and training.

AR and VR technologies can be used to create enhanced online training simulations that completely immerse learners in a virtual situation, eliminating distractions and providing a more engaging and effective learning experience. One can build simulations of complex phenomena such as natural disasters, medical procedures, and scientific experiments inside AR, VR, or a combination of both, allowing students to experience and comprehend the information firsthand, deepening their engagement and understanding.

AR and VR technologies are being used to create serious games featuring memorable characters and immersive storylines that enable employees to use all the resources at their disposal to overcome challenges. Feedback is provided that highlights their mistakes, along with tips to improve their performance.

Some new innovations have stretched the possibilities of deep immersion and gamification even further:

Haptic Feedback: This technology provides physical feedback to the user, such as vibration or pressure, to enhance the immersive experience.

Insightful Analytics: AR and VR technologies can feature detailed analytics to track every move of online learners, including their emotional state and level of alertness, via sensors, providing instructors with valuable feedback to improve their teaching methods.

9/ EMERGING TECHNOLOGIES FOR SPEED

If you are able to use these technologies strategically, you may be able to speed up employee learning and shorten TTP drastically.

EIGHT TYPES OF PERFORMANCE SUPPORT SYSTEMS

Managers tend to rely heavily on training and more often underestimate the value of PSSs.

When you make information, knowledge, and learning available to employees JIT at the point of need or at the teachable moment during the job, they can apply them in the context of their jobs. If people could get questions answered at the point of need, that would speed up their on-the-job proficiency way faster. Simple things like job aids, checklists, task sheets, flow charts, procedures, models, algorithms, decision tables, etc. can do wonders in speeding up performance.

PSSs are meant to achieve that goal. PSSs may include a range of electronic resources such as online learning content, reference material, knowledge base, procedures, mobile applications, and decision-making software, which, according to the project leaders, can provide JIT training or support.

The recent pandemic has increased the importance of this technology to the point that it has become the core of most organizational learning endeavors. As we have seen, organizational learning moves from being a training event to which employees need to be invited to something that happens automatically as employees seek assistance on-the-job from PSSs. They are powerful tools that are now used in place of or in the augmentation of training. These are not some tools sitting on the sideline but rather used during the task as part of the workflow.

Incidentally, this is also the space where technologies are evolving at a rapid pace. With the availability of new technologies, the shape and extent of PSSs are also changing beyond their original role of JIT resources for training, support, or information. This is the one single element of the ecosystem that you, as a learning technologist, can rely on if your workforce is geographically dispersed. When in-person training is not feasible or when training itself does not give you results in terms of faster readiness of your teams, then you need to implement PSSs strategically to provide employees with PSSs that can provide JIT coaching and mentoring.

My research suggests eight types of PSSs, as shown in Figure 9.3, which are shaping workforce learning and proficiency.

9/ EMERGING TECHNOLOGIES FOR SPEED

Figure 9.3: The eight types of PSSs.

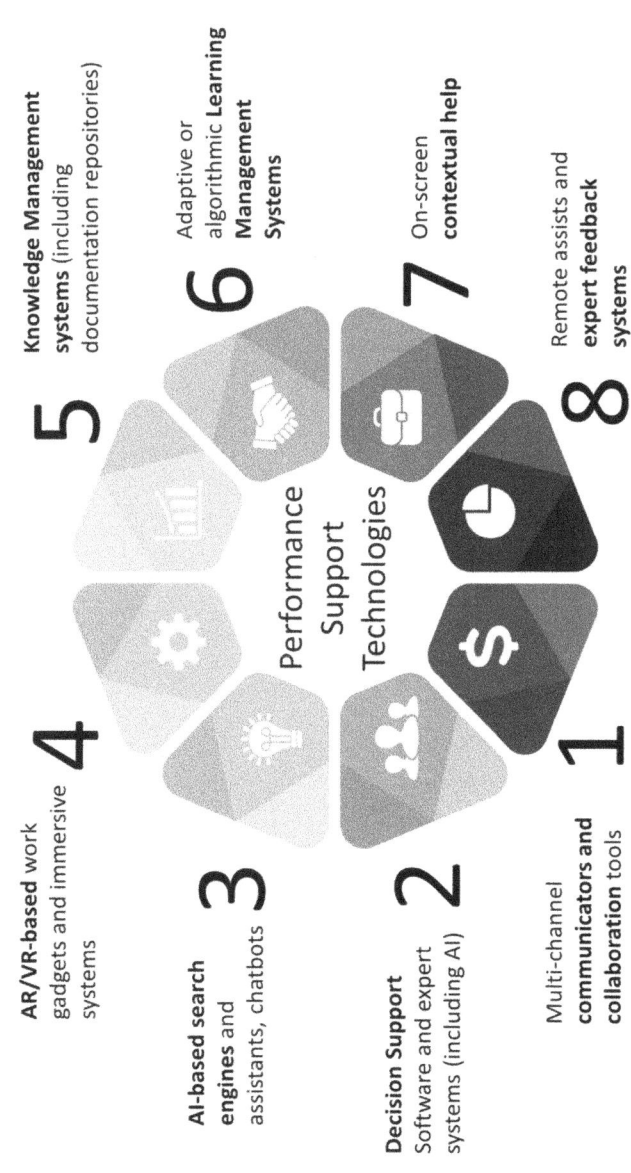

PSSs can be simply a learning delivery resource like LMS, where one can get self-paced content and on-demand videos. It may be a document repository of the organization or simply a repository of YouTube-type videos. The primary goal is to get learning on-demand JIT when someone needs it. As simple as checklists or job aids to more sophisticated ones like AR-based job instructions, contextual on-screen help, decision-support software, and AI-based search engines. Others may include more straightforward but easy-to-implement, like on-the-go push notifications, mobile apps, chatbots, skill self-assessments and procedures, and manuals.

1. Multichannel communicators and Collaboration tools

Most basic forms of PSS technologies include multichannel communicators such as Skype, Teams, Slacks, and Twilio, among others, to instantly connect with anyone to ask questions or help.

2. Decision-support and expert systems

Decision-support systems are software or expert systems to support executives, leaders, and managers in making quick and accurate decisions based on data or qualitative inferences. These systems range from dashboard-based analytics to data visualization tools to AI-driven data insights.

Here are some leading examples:

IBM Watson Analytics[37]: IBM Watson Analytics is a cloud-based data analysis and visualization platform. It is used to help executives

---

[37] https://www.ibm.com/cloud/watson-studio

9/ EMERGING TECHNOLOGIES FOR SPEED

make quicker and more effective decisions based on several parameters. Such a system can help organizations identify patterns and insights in their data. It can be used to help employees make better decisions by providing them with real-time insights and predictions based on the data they are working with.

Three industry-leading software, as examples of decision-support systems are *TIBCO Spotfire*[38], *SAP Lumira*[39] and *QlikView*[40] offering largely similar capabilities. All of these, are BI and analytics software that can help organizations make better decisions by providing them with real-time data visualizations and insights. These can be used to analyze data from multiple sources, including spreadsheets, databases, and cloud-based applications, and can help employees identify patterns and trends in their data.

Microsoft Power BI[41]: Microsoft Power BI is a business analytics service that provides interactive visualizations and BI capabilities with an interface simple enough for end users to create their own reports and dashboards. Power BI is cloud-based and can be used to analyze data from a wide range of sources, including Excel spreadsheets, on-premises and cloud-based data sources, and other cloud-based applications.

Decision-support software can be an incredibly powerful tool for enhancing employee performance. By providing employees with real-time data insights and predictions, they can make informed decisions that can help them achieve their goals and improve their overall performance.

---

[38] https://www.tibco.com/products/tibco-spotfire
[39] https://www.sap.com/products/technology-platform/lumira.html
[40] https://www.qlik.com/us/
[41] https://powerbi.microsoft.com/en-us/

3. Advanced AI-based search engines and assistants

AI-based search engines allow employees to quickly and precisely find what they need depending on the context of the case or problem, or customer issues; for example, documentation, specification, product details, how-to video, or anything from corporate repositories.

There are several excellent examples of AI-based search engines available today. They are becoming increasingly popular due to their ability to provide personalized and relevant search results. While some are simply powerful search engineers, others are context-based chatbots that can help your employees get precise answers to business information.

Here are some of the most notable ones:

ChatGPT[42]: An AI chatbot from OpenAI, this revolutionary tool can answer a wide range of questions and provide information on various topics. Lately, it has been integrated into Microsoft's Bing search engine and in Microsoft Co-pilot[43], providing personalized search results, suggestions, and visual search features and extending the capabilities of Microsoft apps. As a learning technologist, you can draw upon its power by connecting API to your organization's knowledge repository and teaching AI about your know-how.

Google Bard/Gemini[44]: Google's another powerful AI assistant can work in standalone mode as well as integrated in Google applications and search engines, providing multimodal assistance to the users.

---

[42] https://chat.openai.com/
[43] https://www.microsoft.com/en-us/microsoft-copilot
[44] https://gemini.google.com/app

9/ EMERGING TECHNOLOGIES FOR SPEED

IBM Watson AI assistance[45]: This AI assistant from IBM is a natural language chatbot. It can help your employees to deliver exceptional customer experiences that are faster and more accurate. The chatbot understands your customers' queries in context so your employees can deliver fast, consistent, and accurate solutions when and where your customers need them.

Hundreds of new AI chatbots and search engineers are evolving daily. Tall claims, as well as some compelling results, are being demonstrated by some of the latest chatbots like YouChat[46], Perplexity[47], Algolia AI[48], and several new players are growing this list every day. These chatbots offer a combination of features, including summarized results and cited sources for search results.

Remember that the power of these search engines is leveraged when integrated into your organization's technological infrastructure over documentation repositories, knowledge bases, video libraries, and other intellectual properties that need to be processed to draw quick insights.

4. AR- and VR-based gadgets

In the previous section, I explained the application of AR and VR gadgets as learning technologies. However, AR and VR are far more impactful as performance support technologies. These are setting

---

[45] https://www.ibm.com/products/watson-assistant
[46] https://you.com/
[47] https://perplexity.ai/
[48] https://www.algolia.com/products/ai-search

standards for rethinking learning, social, and performance technologies.

The underlying philosophy of AR/VR technology is simple. If you get precise, contextual instructions on what to do at a given point, it shortens the time to training and allows you to be productive independently faster. Using an augmented headset, employees can access instructions, videos, or other help while working on a task with their hands. They don't have to look for manuals or papers. It does not restrict the vision; it superimposes work instructions onto employees' normal vision while keeping hands free for doing complex tasks. AR headsets can support tons of different media to make work highly successful, like even pointing out errors to the employees in real-time. Those instructions are JIT during the workflow. It has seen much success in shortening TTP in complex tasks like building products or repairing equipment.

Here are some great examples of AR-based PSSs:

Employee onboarding: Companies can use AR technology to create interactive department signs that guide new employees to learn more about the office and the people who work there.

Industrial uses: AR smart glasses can be used in manufacturing, warehousing, and field service environments to provide workers with real-time information and support while they perform their tasks.

Technical support: AR can be used as a performance support tool during the workflow to do a task. For example, in complex field services domains such as the repair of machines, maintenance, troubleshooting, equipment, and power stations, AR/VR hands-free headsets are changing the way we bring field service engineers up-to speed. It can provide technicians with step-by-step instructions on repairing a machine or troubleshooting an issue. The headsets allow them to access step-by-step instructors and resources to resolve a problem. With such technologies, you can pretty much put a field service staff into the field with minimal training and let the rest happen onsite.

Customer service: Companies like CSS Corp offer AR solutions that can transform customer experience and cut operating costs by providing intelligent visual support.

5. Knowledge management systems and Documentation repositories

Knowledge capture and management are other kinds of systems that are widely used as e-learning resources. Document management tools help organizations improve efficiency and productivity by making access to information and sharing of information easier. Knowledge management systems could either augment or completely replace the training interventions if strategically deployed. For instance, it can be your document repository. When field staff can access that knowledge precisely at the point of need, it can significantly influence the speed at which they can come up-to the required speed. Some service operations have decision-support software on the field staff's tablets or smartphones that guides them through the customer cases.

Arnold & Collier[49] (2013) demonstrated that e-learning systems designed using knowledge management around an expert system and case-based e-learning accelerated the expertise of new financial

---

[49] Arnold, V., P. Collier, S. Leech, S. Sutton, and A. Vincent, 2013, INCASE: Simulating experience to accelerate expertise development by knowledge workers, International Journal of Intelligent Systems in Accounting, Finance and Management 20, 1–21.

analysts, providing highly complex decision-making to business corporations without actually requiring any training.

Knowledge management systems have become robust online learning platforms by integrating learning material (such as scenario-based questions) into business procedures. Additionally, if integrated with an LMS, you can track employee progress through the procedure-based exercises that they must complete to achieve and prove competence. Such a technology strategy provides a comprehensive map of organizational learning and competence.

6. On-demand and JIT learning

Taking information-oriented content and making it available to employees as self-guided online searchable content can ensure JIT access. Such JIT knowledge access at the point of need makes a huge difference in learning what you need, when you need it, and as much as you need. It saves a lot of time!

It is suggested that the content be taken out from instructor-led sessions and made accessible through PSSs as self-paced learning activities to prepare the learners. By doing so, employees can access the resources at their own pace rather than at the instructor's pace, significantly reducing the time from the proficiency cycle. This makes good use of the learner's time while waiting for the instructor-led session and allows the formal training intervention to focus more on critical and complex hands-on skills.

An attempt to remove unnecessary informational content from the training modules can lead to a shorter training time.

9/ EMERGING TECHNOLOGIES FOR SPEED

There is a trend to use electronic PSSs to provide individualized online access instead of upfront information content-heavy training. Learners can use or access content based on the need of the task at hand rather than learning it beforehand. By using PSS to deliver informational content, the formal training intervention can focus more on critical human skills required for proficiency. One of the reasons that PSS is able to accelerate proficiency is its ability to reinforce learning and knowledge at specified intervals.

The new LMS systems are becoming powerful now with the unmatchable capability to provide on-demand informational content, procedures, documents, videos, and web-based training at the time of need. Component Content Management Systems (CCMS) systems now integrate content and training into one platform, making on-demand learning much more efficient. Mobile-enabled CCMS and content delivery systems have broken the boundaries of jobs and are now able to provide on-demand learning on the go or directly at the job.

7. Contextual on-screen help

A large financial services call center in the US used to provide 11 weeks of instructor-led training to its agents. They found that the agents will take an additional 3 months to become fully proficient. They then implemented a technology that identified where an employee was on the screen or step and then provided contextual help to employees, like what to check and what questions to ask from the customer. The software provided decision-making, like how and when to escalate the call to others. By providing the basic orientation to the software and remaining moved as PSS on their screen, the company was able to reduce TTP by almost 70%. The software basically completely eliminated the training for the most part.

Such software appears directly within the application interface to help users complete tasks or overcome issues that they are likely to encounter and then provide users with real-time support while using a software application. Here are some great examples of on-screen contextual help software:

KnowledgeOwl[50]: This contextual help solution is designed to appear within the application interface when users need it the most. This solution is meant to reduce the need for users to refer to manuals or support documents when they encounter an issue while using an application.

ScreenSteps[51]: This context-sensitive help browser extension is a tool that puts training and reference documents directly into the web application where employees need them. With this tool, users no longer have to search endless tabs or documents to find the necessary information.

Userlane[52]: This software allows companies to measure how employees use applications, identify areas for improvement, and create on-screen interactive guides and tours for software. This solution aims to enable users to immediately use any software without needing instructions or training.

Microsoft Power Automate[53]: This software provides in-product contextual help that displays content that is relevant to the currently selected action, trigger, or connector. When users display the in-product help, they can select any link from the list of help topics, and the corresponding documentation will open.

---

[50] https://www.knowledgeowl.com/features/
[51] https://www.screensteps.com/
[52] https://www.userlane.com/platform/context-sensitive-help/
[53] https://powerautomate.microsoft.com/en-us/

9/ EMERGING TECHNOLOGIES FOR SPEED

OnScreen[54]: This software that digitizes existing documentation and converts content into in-app walkthroughs. This solution is designed to help users onboard and refresh their knowledge with the context provided by world-class trainers.

These are just a few examples of on-screen contextual help software that helps users navigate software applications more quickly and efficiently. However, keep in mind that, though such applications improve efficiency, shortening TTP should remain the end goal.

8. Remote assists and expert feedback

Some of the latest technologies allow employees to seek remote assistance from experts in real time when stuck at work. For instance, plant and equipment repair technicians use AR headsets with built-in remote capabilities to pull relevant experts into the scene remotely when needed. The experts on the other side of the globe can see what these technicians see in real time. There are real-time conversations, discussions, and collaborative troubleshooting. Research tells us that with such instant feedback, JIT coaching hugely accelerates the TTP.

Also, such technologies allow for building a network of coaches from different corners with different sets of expertise. Research shows that having multiple coaches with diverse experience when tapped correctly, could help employees master new behaviors quickly.

The advantage is that you don't have to wait for an employee to be 100% ready in training on everything before you can use them to support field issues. These augmented expert systems, which are

---

[54]https://onscreen.us/onscreen-for-web-apps/

remote-assisted technologies, provide them with performance support when they really need it.

Strategic thinking for implementing PSS techs

When you apply the PSS strategy, you are not pushing or forcing employees to learn. Instead, you are looking for what is available to them when they are doing a job or what new tools can be made available that either reduce or eliminate the training requirement. While your training designers design online training, you need to ask, "What skills can be delivered more effectively through PSSs as JIT learning or support instead of needing training events?" The result could be highly targeted and much shorter training while relying heavily on PSSs as the first line of defense. As a learning technologist, remember that the real impact of PSSs is seen when integrated into the workflow.

FOUR TYPES OF SOCIAL TECHNOLOGIES

What do you do when you get into a problem or forget something? You ask your buddy in the next cubicle or someone on the phone. And you get things solved fast by talking to others! Imagine how much wait time is cut out in your journey to produce outcomes and become proficient.

9/ EMERGING TECHNOLOGIES FOR SPEED

Figure 9.4: Social technologies.

That is where technologies like instant communicators, collaboration platforms, expert directories, or even community of practices platforms are highly useful. Their relevance has become even more important post-pandemic because people don't sit next to each other. These techs can be integrated into Outlook, Teams, mobile apps, and other enterprise devices.

In my observation, implementing social technologies is probably the most overlooked action in organizations. As a leader, you have to make sure that you have a strategy behind how these social technologies are deployed. In fact, too many of these may be even a distraction to productivity if a proper strategy is not considered.

Four major categories of social technologies have been making waves. As more and more technologies converge, we see movement toward integrating all four technology categories into one platform. The closest example of such convergence is the IBM Connections Engagement Suite[55]. If applied strategically, you can shorten TTP of your employees.

1. *Real-time collaboration tools*
2. *Expert directories*
3. *Community of practice platforms*
4. *Multichannel communicators*

1. Real-time collaboration tools

For a moment, think about how the work is typically done in the teams in any organization. It involves group work, collaboration, exchange, and feedback. There is a multi-pronged evaluation by various stakeholders during the workflow till a perfect outcome is achieved.

If you could incorporate all those work dynamics and social interactions into a suitable technology, you could hasten employees' learning curve, apart from being efficient. All that can be achieved in the new world using real-time collaboration technologies. These technologies allow individuals and teams to work together seamlessly in real time, regardless of their physical location. These

---

[55] IBM Connections Engagement Suite offers an integrated set of solutions for increasing employee engagement, collaboration, and productivity.
https://www.ibm.com/common/ssi/ShowDoc.wss?docURL=/common/ssi/rep_ca/5/897/ENUS217-535/index.html&lang=en&request_locale=en

technologies are either project-driven, team-driven, or function-driven. In the end, the goal of any implementation is to enable real-time work with each other, start conversations, and keep it going.

Platforms such as Zoom, Skype, and Google Meet enable remote teams to have real-time face-to-face meetings, reducing travel costs and improving communication. Most collaboration tools have built-in communicators. For instance, Slack and Microsoft Teams enable real-time text communication, allowing teams to stay connected and collaborate more efficiently. Collaboration tools include desktop-sharing features that enable remote teams to view and control each other's screens, facilitating remote troubleshooting and training.

On top of that, most collaborators support features similar to Microsoft Whiteboard or Zoom Whiteboard in order to enable their teams to collaborate on visual projects in real time, allowing for remote brainstorming and ideation. The collaborations are enhanced with cloud-based document editing and sharing tools such as Google Drive, Dropbox Paper, and Microsoft SharePoint, allowing teams to collaborate on documents in real time.

Real-time collaboration technologies have become essential tools for modern workplaces, especially those with distributed or remote teams. These technologies help improve efficiency, productivity, and team collaboration by enabling seamless communication and collaboration.

2. Expert directories

An internal expert directory is a tool used by organizations to identify and leverage the expertise of their employees. Behind those technologies are the well-managed, cloud-based databases of experts and employees in terms of who has done what, who has worked with large customers, and who has won large deals. Imagine how powerful would that kind of know-how be. Your employees can go to that person immediately to seek tips to shorten their journeys. Otherwise, they would have to start from scratch.

Expert directories allow project teams, work groups, departments, communities, and employees across the enterprise to find the expertise resident in their organizations. Often, expert directories include experts from external sources.

Not many companies do a good job of building fully validated, up-to-date, accomplishment-based expert directories with social connectivity and collaboration functions. More often, companies maintain directories highlighting the experiences and skills of experts rather than building a portfolio of their accomplishments, projects, and results. Massive effort is required to identify the expertise taxonomy and then apply a granular taxonomy to each job role in the company.

From a technology procurement and implementation standpoint, there is no one single approach to expertise locators. Stan Garfield[56], a noted knowledge management author and speaker, has revealed some great recommendations for various approaches in his article. Expertise databases can be self-filled by employees so that they can project their skills and accomplishments and be more discoverable. Alternatively, HR can fill the database based on what they know, or the system may be able to pull available data from repositories like LinkedIn. Good expertise locators will incorporate rich metadata schemas of job titles, organizational structures, company-specific

---

[56]Garfield, S. 2021. Expertise Locators and Ask the Expert. https://lucidea.com/blog/km-component-35-expertise-locators-and-ask-the-expert/

9/ EMERGING TECHNOLOGIES FOR SPEED

terminologies, business processes, content taxonomies, etc., to provide highly accurate results.

People can quickly find the experts they need to solve problems and stop wasting time looking for information. Garfield suggests that the next level approach is to use a social profile method, which includes self-tagging, peer tagging, or rating. This could allow employees to search for colleagues by name, job title, location, and expertise. Another possible way is to implement crawlers into work-related content, contributed content, or community discussions. Such an expertise locator can provide information on employees' experience, publications, and other relevant information. Above all, a searchable option is required to search for expertise and locate experts in context. With that, the expertise locator tool enables employees to search for colleagues with specific skills or knowledge. This can allow project teams and work groups to access and utilize this expertise.

In conclusion, organizations use internal expert directories to leverage the knowledge and skills of their employees. IBM, Deloitte, Cisco, Microsoft, and Siemens are examples of companies deploying such tools.

3. Community of practices platforms

A large IT company practiced a Friday afternoon pizza hour for several weeks. They would gather their high performers and new performers together, eat, and share information on a specific topic facilitated by the person who sets the agenda. This simple act does something wonderful. It allows new performers to access the high performers who may have solved a similar problem and will quickly guide these new team members. They connect and learn from the master performer rather than waiting for formal training classes or relying on unmanaged informal learning. This is an example of purpose-driven social connectivity. Now, if you can implement the platforms and technologies to enable similar kinds of connectivity and networks, you may be able to speed up TTP.

The reality is that employees work with each other to produce results as a group. They don't work in isolation! There are usual team interactions from which they learn socially and informally. They do so by coworking with each other, talking to each other, sharing with others, and supporting each other. These interactions act as a powerful multiplier of skill or competency.

That is why the social techs, called the Communities of Practice (CoP) platforms, significantly impact speed. These platforms allow people at work to create groups and purpose-driven networks on specific topics, issues, or functions.

CoP platforms are a great way for organizations to increase employee social interactions and promote knowledge sharing and collaboration. For instance, Yammer[57] and Jive[58] are examples of private social networks for businesses that allow employees to collaborate and communicate in a secure online environment. They provide a platform for CoPs where employees can share knowledge, discuss ideas, and ask questions. CoP platforms like Slack[59], Confluence[60], and Microsoft Teams[61] are team communication and collaboration platforms that allow employees to connect and work together in real time.

---

[57] https://www.microsoft.com/en-us/microsoft-365/yammer/yammer-overview
[58] https://www.jivesoftware.com/
[59] https://slack.com/
[60] https://www.atlassian.com/software/confluence
[61] https://www.microsoft.com/en-ww/microsoft-teams/teams-for-work

9/ EMERGING TECHNOLOGIES FOR SPEED

As an executive or leader of the organization, you need to figure out the right technology or platform for setting up learning networks for specific purposes—it may be based on projects or functions or the tenure of the employees. In fact, for every new hire, there should be a defined network to start with. Tools such as Microsoft Teams and Slack allow you to have some features to create groups and networks. And, when done right, you achieve this without sacrificing productivity. Rather, you will add speed to performance. The technologies that allow embedding purpose-driven discussions, conversations, and interactions among the performers in these networks would actually help toward speeding up proficiency.

However, care must be taken to ensure that such technologies do not become another file-dump system or email alternative. If you need to make a difference with these technologies, there must be a targeted knowledge creation that can be fed back to new people to accelerate their proficiency. For instance, if you have a network on the best practices on risk assessment, make sure refined knowledge is created, shared, and made as a corporate culture, like how things should happen moving forward.

4. Multichannel communicators

Multichannel communicators are tools and platforms that allow for communication across multiple channels, such as email, SMS, social media, and chat. Several years ago, separate technologies or standalone applications were required to be integrated into a company's infrastructure. However, with the convergence of technologies, such communicators are built into the LMSs, PSSs, and CoP platforms.

For instance, Twilio[62], a cloud communications platform, allows businesses to build messaging, voice, and video into their apps using APIs. It includes channels like SMS, voice, video, chat, and WhatsApp. CRM systems like HubSpot[63] and Salesforce[64] not only include a range of tools for sales, marketing, and customer service but also support multichannel communication tools such as email marketing, SMS, live chat, and social media management. Slack[65] is another messaging platform designed for team communication through various channels, including direct messaging, group messaging, and channels.

Other enterprise systems like Microsoft Teams, Zoom, WhatsApp Business, and Facebook support powerful communicators, including messaging, video calls, voice calls, and file sharing.

Choosing the right multichannel communicator for your organization depends on your specific needs and the channels your customers prefer to communicate through.

AI-BASED E-LEARNING PLATFORMS AND TOOLS

AI-based e-learning, also known as intelligent e-learning, refers to the use of AI technologies to enhance the effectiveness and efficiency of e-learning. More recently, ChatGPT and Gemini, among other derivative AI tools, have stormed the market as next-generation e-learning tools. Admittedly, these can cut off a large percentage of

---

[62]https://www.twilio.com/
[63]https://www.hubspot.com/
[64]https://www.salesforce.com/
[65]https://slack.com/

9/ EMERGING TECHNOLOGIES FOR SPEED

your time as a content developer, but how would it ensure the shortening of the TTP of your learners?

Your content development cycle might become efficient, but unless you apply it in such a way that makes learners' proficiency faster, it has no big impact.

Thus, you must be careful about what is a tool and what is a strategy. For instance, 'push assessment on the go' can be a strategy, while specific mobile apps supporting such a strategy are endless. However, you still need a larger strategy to leverage such tools strategically to accelerate learning.

Some possibilities to enhance your e-learning based on AI are as follows. Also, check the framework in the bonus section to understand how to apply consumer AI tools to transform enterprise L&D:

AI-based personalized learning path

With the advent of AI, e-learning platforms are becoming more intelligent and personalized, providing students with a unique learning experience that is tailored to their needs and preferences. AI algorithms can analyze student data and identify their strengths and weaknesses, enabling them to provide a customized learning experience. Personalized learning paths ensure that students are presented with relevant content at the right time, increasing the effectiveness of the learning process. Companies like Coursera have used this approach, which leverages AI to provide learners with personalized recommendations on what courses to take next based on their previous learning activities.

AI can also personalize learning paths by determining appropriate content for each learner based on their level of comprehension and preferred modes of learning[66].

AI-based practice for the learners

Another way that AI can be used in e-learning is by using it to create chatbot experiences for learners to practice real-time conversations. Language learning platforms like Duolingo[67] use NLP to create chatbot experiences, allowing language learners to practice their skills and gain confidence before interacting with a real person[68]. The chatbot also provides immediate feedback, allowing learners to identify their mistakes and improve their skills.

Another application of AI is analyzing student data to identify patterns and trends that can be used to improve curriculum and teaching methods[69].

AI-based learning content development

AI can also be used to enhance content development by generating insights from the data gathered from e-learning platforms. With AI, e-learning platforms can analyze large amounts of data to identify patterns and trends that can be used to improve the curriculum and teaching methods. This can lead to the creation of more engaging and relevant learning materials that are better suited to learners' needs.

---

[66]Murtaza et al. 2022. AI-based personalized e-learning systems: Issues, Challenges, and Solutions. Vol 10. 81323-81242. https://ieeexplore.ieee.org/document/9840390/

[67]https://www.duolingo.com/

[68]Learndash. 2020. 4 examples of Ai being Used In E-learning. https://www.learndash.com/4-examples-of-ai-being-used-in-e-learning/

[69]Michelle, E. 2023. Use of AI in eLearning. https://elearningindustry.com/use-of-ai-in-elearning

9/ EMERGING TECHNOLOGIES FOR SPEED

AI-based tutors

AI-based e-learning platforms can also act as a tutor by providing real-time answers to questions raised by students. Learners often face difficulties getting clarification on specific subject matters while learning is going on. AI-based platforms can offer solutions by providing real-time answers to student questions. AI-driven solutions can answer learners' questions, recommend personalized resources, and grade papers (Colorwhistle, 2023)[70]. AI technologies can also be used to teach students about AI itself through hands-on learning experiences and resources for educators (Intel, 2023)[71].

AI-based resources

AI can also make e-learning more accessible to everyone. AI-driven solutions can recommend personalized resources, grade papers, and answer learners' questions. This has been implemented in e-learning platforms like Khan Academy[72], which uses AI to provide personalized recommendations for learners.

Overall, AI-based e-learning offers many possibilities to enhance the effectiveness and efficiency of e-learning solutions. By personalizing learning paths, providing real-time feedback, and offering adaptive learning opportunities, AI can improve learners' engagement, satisfaction, and outcomes.

---

[70] https://colorwhistle.com/impact-of-ai-in-elearning-industry/
[71] https://www.intel.com/content/dam/www/central-libraries/us/en/documents/2023-10/ai-in-education-whitepaper.pdf
[72] https://blog.khanacademy.org/new-khanmigo-interests/

Chapter 1
DIGITAL REVOLUTION IN LEARNING TECHNOLOGIES

Chapter 2
BUSINESS KPIs FOR LEARNING TECHNOLOGY

Chapter 3
STRATEGIC LEARNING TECHNOLOGY LEADERSHIP THINKING

Chapter 4
TECHNOLOGIES & ANALYTICS FOR HIRING RIGHT

Chapter 5
TECHNOLOGIES & ANALYTICS FOR PROFICIENCY METRICS

Chapter 6
TECHNOLOGIES & ANALYTICS FOR WORK SKILLS

Chapter 7
TECHNOLOGIES & ANALYTICS FOR EFFICIENT LEARNING PATH

Chapter 8
TECHNOLOGIES & ANALYTICS FOR TIME MEASUREMENTS

Chapter 9
EMERGING TECHNOLOGIES FOR SPEED

Chapter 10
THE FINAL THOUGHTS

BONUS
MODELLING GEN-AI FOR ENTERPRSE L&D

L&D CAREER RESOURCES

10
FINAL THOUGHTS

10/ FINAL THOUGHTS

To wrap up, irrespective of the technology you choose to use, you need to choose the technology by applying the following five strategies and evaluate the new technology consciously:

1. Look at the capabilities of technologies from a workforce capability and the acceleration you need to provide.
2. Pay attention to the overall learning landscape in the organization.
3. Assess the support systems in the organization and how new technologies can help you fill the gap.
4. Scan how your teams leverage social connectivity and how technologies can accelerate development through those interactions.
5. Once you orchestrate these in an integrated fashion, you need to keep humans (employees) at the center to get a substantial competitive advantage in terms of accelerating your workforce.

Figure 10.1: Five strategies for technology implementation.

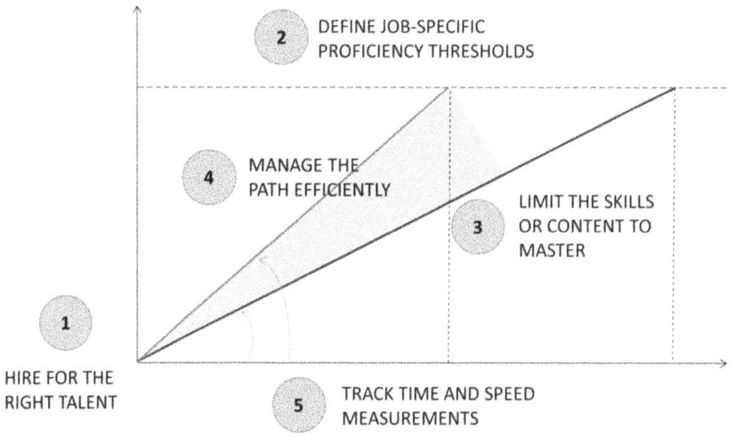

STRATEGIC LEARNING TECHNOLOGY LEADERSHIP

As organizations adopt new technologies, several factors need to be considered, including the capabilities of the technology, the organization's learning landscape, support systems, and how teams leverage social connectivity.

Look at workforce capability and the acceleration needs

First of all, decision-makers must carefully evaluate and introduce new technologies to avoid negative impacts on productivity and efficiency. More often, new technologies don't always make processes or workflows more efficient than before. Sometimes, things may go south on efficiency because you change even your most stable and proven workflow to fit the technologies into corporate functioning. This could potentially be more damaging when technology is introduced to look 'cool' or 'trendy.' Instead, as an executive or decision-maker, focus beyond the use of technology to enable employees to do the work faster or get more work done. Instead, focus on how new technology can accelerate the path to proficiency. Evaluate if the proposed learning technology will truly enhance productivity and accelerate the workforce's proficiency. Thus, you need to assess the workforce capabilities and the required acceleration to provide value to the organization.

Pay attention to the overall learning landscape

Additionally, it is essential to look at the overall learning landscape in the organization to ensure that the new technology is effectively integrated into the existing processes.

Assess the support systems

Furthermore, it is crucial to assess the support systems in the organization and determine how new technologies can fill any gaps in these systems. This includes evaluating the current processes and

10/ FINAL THOUGHTS

workflows to ensure that the new technology is not disrupting the established systems that have proven to be efficient.

Assess team dynamics and connectivity

It is also important to consider how teams leverage social connectivity and how technologies can accelerate development through those interactions. Decision-makers should evaluate how the new technology can help teams collaborate and communicate more effectively, which can ultimately lead to increased productivity.

Keep humans at the center

In the end, keep in mind that you need to keep humans at the center. After all, any technology you introduce is for them. Ironically, we have become too tech-savvy that we forget humans out of the equation. Technology needs to give employees a sense of achievement, a sense of accomplishment, a sense of completing a task more efficiently and productively, a sense of belongingness, and a sense of speed. How you select and implement technology to develop your workforce shows you care for them. When you do so, the workforce will be more productive, and the organization will gain a competitive advantage.

TAKING IT FORWARD

In the last five chapters, you learned a strategic leadership thinking framework consisting of five strategies to implement strategies that can give your organization a competitive edge in the market.

By selecting and implementing technology to speed up the development of workforce skills, performance, and proficiency, you, as a strategic learning technology leader, can demonstrate your commitment to caring for employees.

Use the space below to reflect upon and develop an action plan for each of the five strategies to implement strategic technologies in your context. Review the action plan with your executives. Start incorporating one element at a time in your annual strategic plans. Institute a culture of 'speed' in your organization and be a change agent to educate management staff to speak the language of *time-to-proficiency*. Once you accomplish that, it will be far easier for you to win any ROI battle and stay as a leader who is ahead of technology.

10/ FINAL THOUGHTS

Reflections 10.1

Strategy #1: Hiring right

Action plan:

Strategy #2: Specific proficiency metrics

Action plan:

Strategy #3: Work skills that matter

Action plan:

Strategy #4: Efficient learning path

Action plan:

Strategy #5: Time measurements
Action plan:
Overall system implementation, including ecosystem:
Key things to focus on this year:
Key things to focus on in the next year:
Your plan to accelerate your strategic learning technology leadership:

Chapter 1
DIGITAL REVOLUTION IN LEARNING TECHNOLOGIES

Chapter 2
BUSINESS KPIs FOR LEARNING TECHNOLOGY

Chapter 3
STRATEGIC LEARNING TECHNOLOGY LEADERSHIP THINKING

Chapter 4
TECHNOLOGIES & ANALYTICS FOR HIRING RIGHT

Chapter 5
TECHNOLOGIES & ANALYTICS FOR PROFICIENCY METRICS

Chapter 6
TECHNOLOGIES & ANALYTICS FOR WORK SKILLS

Chapter 7
TECHNOLOGIES & ANALYTICS FOR EFFICIENT LEARNING PATH

Chapter 8
TECHNOLOGIES & ANALYTICS FOR TIME MEASUREMENTS

Chapter 9
EMERGING TECHNOLOGIES FOR SPEED

Chapter 10
THE FINAL THOUGHTS

BONUS
MODELLING GEN-AI FOR ENTERPRSE L&D

L&D CAREER RESOURCES

11
MODELING GEN-AI FOR ENTERPRISE L&D

BONUS 11 / MODELING GEN-AI FOR ENTERPRISE L&D

Note: This bonus content, originally published in an academic magazine, is adapted and provided here as a bonus job aid for AI learning technology strategists.

CONSUMER GEN-AI APPLIED TO L&D

Artificial intelligence and its applications are not novel developments. They have been in existence for several decades. However, with the advent of GenAI, such as ChatGPT[73], Google Gemini[74], Microsoft Co-pilot[75], and Claude[76], among others, understanding human language as a mode of interaction has become a reality. ChatGPT has chartered a revolutionary path with its hyper-realistic level of natural language processing, far beyond rule-based AI systems like IBM Watson. In addition to the other GenAI tools mentioned above, ChatGPT can make sense of the context in which questions are asked, allowing for a natural conversation. This capability enables users to easily interact with GenAI using human language.

Given that ChatGPT or other GenAIs are content-based tools, they have great applications in L&D and training development areas. Creating a training course using traditional instructional design processes can be quite time-consuming. On the contrary, using GenAI can be a massive time-saver for course designers and educators. It quickly creates the structure and content for a course, as well as assessments and quizzes. Several solopreneurs, consultants, and influencers have shown early examples of using the

---

[73] https://chat.openai.com
[74] https://gemini.google.com
[75] https://copilot.microsoft.com
[76] https://claude.ai

free or paid consumer versions of ChatGPT (Model 3.5 or 4.0) to quickly create their course content for small-scale coaching or training projects.

However, applying GenAI to enterprise learning is a different ball game. Over the past year, there have been several powerful use cases of GenAI in the L&D space. Some of these are as follows:

- AI-driven instructional material development[77]
- AI-driven course outline and structure[78]
- AI-driven training video creation[79]
- Data analytics and predictive models[80,81]
- 2D-3D visualization and animation[82]
- AI Augmentation for AR/VR[83]
- AI-personalized learning path[84]
- Training, course management, and scheduling

---

[77] eLearning Industry (2023, Aug 17). The Role Of Artificial Intelligence In Instructional Design. https://elearningindustry.com/role-of-artificial-intelligence-in-instructional-design
[78] Future1st (2023, June 18). *How to Create a Structured Training Program for Your Trainees.* https://www.future1st.com.au/post/how-to-create-a-structured-training-program-for-your-trainees
[79] Hylenski, P (2024). Revolutionizing Training with AI-Created Videos, LinkedIn newsletter, https://www.linkedin.com/pulse/revolutionizing-training-ai-created-videos-paul-hylenski-jaeve/
[80] Forbes (2024, Feb). Revolutionizing Business Decision-Making: The Impact Of Generative AI On Predictive Analytics. https://www.forbes.com/sites/forbestechcouncil/2024/02/23/revolutionizing-business-decision-making-the-impact-of-generative-ai-on-predictive-analytics/
[81] Gad-Elrab, A. A. (2021). Modern business intelligence: Big data analytics and artificial intelligence for creating the data-driven value. In E-Business-Higher Education and Intelligence Applications, Wu, R & Mircea, M (eds.), 135, Intech Open, https://www.intechopen.com/chapters/76332
[82] NVIDIA Omniverse (2023, Sep). How AI-Generated 3D Models are Transforming 3D Pipelines. https://medium.com/@nvidiaomniverse/how-ai-generated-3d-models-are-transforming-3d-pipelines-d4245566a289
[83] FxM web (2024, Feb). AI's Pioneering Role: Navigating the Metaverse, VR, and AR Realms. https://www.fxmweb.com/insights/ai-s-pioneering-role-navigating-the-metaverse-vr-and-ar-realms.html
[84] Camola, V., Bansal, G., et al. (2023, July 28). Beyond Reality: The Pivotal Role of Generative AI in the Metaverse - arXiv. https://arxiv.org/abs/2308.06272

- AI performance supports[85]

This paper focuses on the use case of GenAI for the first three items: AI-driven instructional design, training content development, and training videos. In this paper, I demonstrate how L&D professionals can remodel their current enterprise learning and training development process by leveraging the power of ChatGPT (or any other GenAI tools) to efficiently create standard elements in a typical learning program. In the end, the paper provides a 9-step job aid for L&D practitioners to extend GenAI to a range of L&D deliverables while significantly reducing human effort, reducing cost, and accelerating the overall training program design process.

SHOWCASING ENTERPRISE L&D WITH GEN-AI

Let's say you are in charge of designing learning programs for employees. Part of that challenge is to analyze the training needs, availability, and state of current content. This also includes creating course scope and outline, and developing online or offline training material such as presentation slides, assessments, and videos. Moreover, accomplishing all of these tasks takes time.

However, for the sake of simplicity, I describe how you can accomplish each element of typical instructional design, development, and delivery using the free consumer version of ChatGPT (ChatGPT 3.5) and then scale up by implementing enterprise AI tools.

---

[85] Rasheed, Z., Ghwanmeh, S., & Abualkishik, A. Z. (2023). Harnessing Artificial Intelligence for Personalized Learning: A Systematic Review. Data and Metadata. 2,146. https://doi.org/10.56294/dm2023146

For this demonstration, I used ChatGPT 3.5 to build a short in-person training course to teach learners how to understand and apply Microsoft Excel's new function, XLOOKUP, targeted at junior professionals who already know how to use the previous common function, VLOOKUP.

In the following sections, I demonstrate how I trained the ChatGPT model with a custom knowledge base and then prompted it step-by-step to build all the training course components, training content, lesson plans, course outlines, presentation slides, assessments, and videos, as part of the overall training development.

Step 1: Analyzing Training Gaps and Needs

Typical enterprise process: Typically, training specialists look at skills required for a particular job and then review performance data to identify gaps in the current training structure and content. Based on this analysis, they determine certain performance or skill gaps and new training needs. Generally, this leads to determining skills or competencies that must be taught in a new or revised training program. This assessment is usually done manually through back-and-forth conversations with experts by making qualitative references from various sources or inputs. The accuracy of this process is as good as that of the people involved in conducting the gap analysis, besides being highly effort-intensive and subjective. This is where ChatGPT or equivalent GenAI tools come in, as they can perform the analysis objectively and within a few minutes.

Extending GenAI to achieve this Goal: For this demonstration, I scoped my goal only to perform training content gap analysis, which involved analyzing existing training content for potential gaps and ascertaining what additional content should be developed to deliver the identified skills.

I found a slide set on XLOOKUP that was written as a mini-training presentation. I referred to this as 'available training content.'

I used the ChatDocAI[86] tool and HumataAI[87] tool, both of which have the ability to read documents in various formats, such as Word or PowerPoint. I prompted it to analyze the 'available training content.' As shown in Figure 11.1, I provided it with intended learning objectives and asked it to report any information gaps that must be covered in the training course:

Prompt: <*What information should I add to make this document more comprehensive?*>

GenAI suggested adding a more detailed explanation of certain topics. These gaps or suggested topics can then be used to develop complete training material.

Implications for L&D: Training content gap analysis is typically a small step of the bigger training need analysis exercise. This exercise is becoming more data-driven, given that large-scale LMS systems now allow a range of learning analytics. In this case, several new GenAI tools (Popai[88], MindGrasp[89], ChatDoc[90], Viable[91], DocLime[92], etc.) can be handy in analyzing a given set of documents, such as presentation slides, vendor documents, procedures, field data, student performance data, student feedback, reviewer comments, and

---

[86] https://chatdoc.ai
[87] https://humata.ai
[88] https://popai.pro
[89] https://mingrasp.ai
[90] https://chatdoc.ai
[91] https://askviable.com
[92] https://doclime.com

other sources. Based on that, GenAI can identify patterns of skill or performance gaps against the specified learning goals. When automated, such a process can reduce a massive amount of human time.

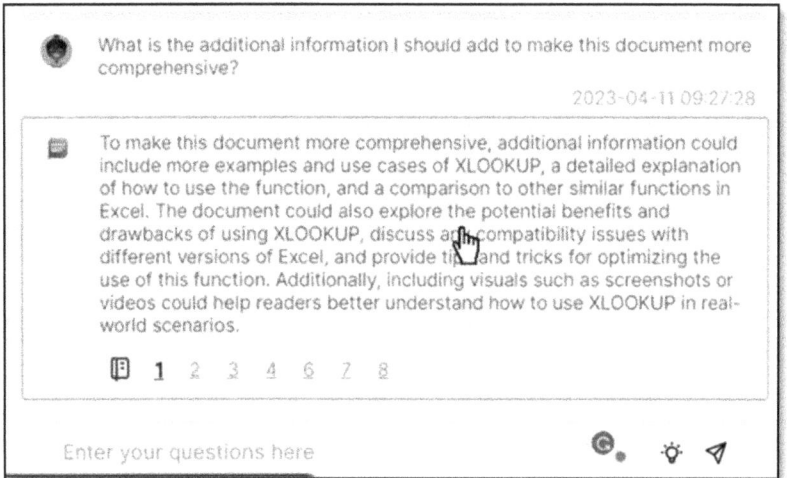

Figure 11.1: ChatDoc input and output to analyze content gaps

Step 2: Creating a Training Outline and Structure

Typical enterprise process: Creating a course outline, modular structure, and module outline is usually the first step in any corporate course creation. Typically, this process involves thoroughly reviewing relevant and available documentation (which may include formal standard operating procedures), field notes, and training gap analysis with stakeholders and consulting them. Like other training development processes, this also requires human intervention and multiple discussions, reviews, and approvals from stakeholders.

Extending GenAI to achieve this goal: GenAI can be utilized to perform that task by leveraging available documentation to create a training course that includes hands-on activities, case examples, quizzes, and assessments. To demonstrate this, I prompted ChatGPT to assume the role of expert course designer to create a course description and outline for the XLOOKUP course. When you provide the GenAI tool with context, the outputs are far more accurate and specific.

Prompt <*You are an expert on course design and you are also an expert on Excel. Your job is to create a training course for professionals who have basic understanding of excel. The course is to teach them XLOOKUP function. The course should have hands-on activities as well as case examples to practice the function.*>

For input documentation, I instructed it to use only the information or content fetched from two XLOOKUP procedures from 2 different URLs. These two URLs outline XLOOKUP function procedures that can act as SOP in this case, based on which training content will be developed. Both procedures are completely distinct, written by different authors, and provide different explanations of XLOOKUP.

Prompt <*Create a course description, outline, and lesson plan for a course on XLOOKUP. Use the information contained in procedures at URLs X and Y to create the outline and content.*>

Figure 1.2: ChatGPT output to create a training outline

Course Outline

Module 1: Introduction to XLOOKUP
- Overview of XLOOKUP function and its features
- Key differences between VLOOKUP and XLOOKUP

Module 2: Basic XLOOKUP Operations
- Setting up data for XLOOKUP
- Syntax of XLOOKUP
- Using XLOOKUP for exact matches
- Using XLOOKUP for partial matches

Module 3: Advanced XLOOKUP Operations
- Using XLOOKUP with wildcard characters
- Using XLOOKUP with multiple criteria
- Using XLOOKUP with multiple return values

Figure 1.3: ChatGPT input and output to create a detailed training outline

Expand the bullets into further details

Sure! Here are some expanded details for each module in the course outline:

Module 1: Introduction to XLOOKUP
- Overview of XLOOKUP function and its features: In this module, we'll start by introducing the XLOOKUP function and discussing its features. We'll talk about how XLOOKUP is different from other lookup functions, such as VLOOKUP and HLOOKUP, and we'll discuss some of the benefits of using XLOOKUP in your work.
- Key differences between VLOOKUP and XLOOKUP: In this section, we'll take a closer look at the differences between VLOOKUP and XLOOKUP. We'll discuss some of the limitations of VLOOKUP and how XLOOKUP addresses these limitations. We'll also talk about when it's appropriate to use VLOOKUP and when it's better to use XLOOKUP.

Within seconds, the AI created a high-level module and sub-bullets for the course, including topics such as advanced XLOOKUP operations, best practices, and case studies, as shown in Figure 1.2. Then, I prompted it to add more details about each bullet point to refine the outline further, as shown in Figure 1.3, and also create a lesson plan.

Implication for L&D: GenAI can be instructed to use a specific set of materials and quickly generate a module outline and a lesson plan. It can create a draft of the training course in a matter of minutes, which can then be refined further by the instructional designer. While the AI's output may need to be revised by a human, the speed with which it creates this intelligence is impressive and could potentially be used to expedite the course creation process.

Step 3: Developing Instructor's Presentation Slides

Typical enterprise process: Most training courses rely on instructor-driven presentation slides, whether in-person or remote training classes, as the primary delivery mechanism. Presentation slides are facilitation tools that can be used to create storyboards for instructor-led videos. Even if a course is self-learning-based, presentation slides are prepared in some form, whether as a script or a storyboard. Given that GenAI tools are content-driven, we believe they hold great promise for swiftly creating the required presentation material.

Extending GenAI to achieve this goal: To demonstrate this feasibility, I prompted ChatGPT to develop an outline of slides by feeding it the course outline I created previously:

Prompt <*I would like you to create an outline for the presentation slides that the instructor can use to teach the above course. Limit to 10 slides maximum. Fill out enough details for bullets and sub-bullets.*>

ChatGPT generated an outline by automatically organizing the content in the form of slides developed in a logical progression. However, it was a little thin in detail.

Then, I prompted it to expand the bullets into detailed content, as shown in Figure 1.4. While the slides may not be the final ones for the training course, they can act as an accelerated headstart for instructional designers to populate and correct the content depending on the program's needs.

Figure 1.4: ChatGPT input and output to create a detailed outline of presentation slides

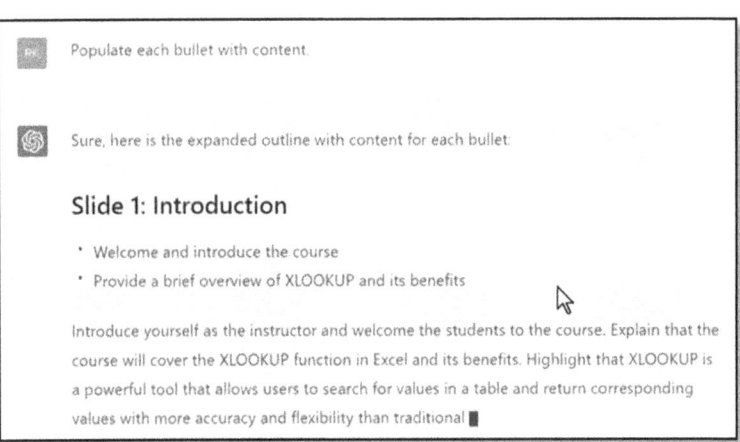

From there, I pasted this ChatGPT-generated outline into another AI tool called GammaAI[93]. Gamma AI is an automated AI

---

[93] https://gamma.ai

BONUS 11 / MODELING GEN-AI FOR ENTERPRISE L&D

tool that converts minimal text or even high-level ideas into full presentations. This tool simply extracts instructions from the content you provide.

The Gamma tool created a full deck of slides instantly based on the context of each bullet point, as shown in Figure 1.5. It also automatically selects appropriate images for the content and context and provides the slides in the most suitable layout to support the goal. The same function can now be done using ChatGPT 4.0 plugins or other AI apps like TomeAI[94].

Figure 1.5: Gamma AI output to create slides from the basic outline

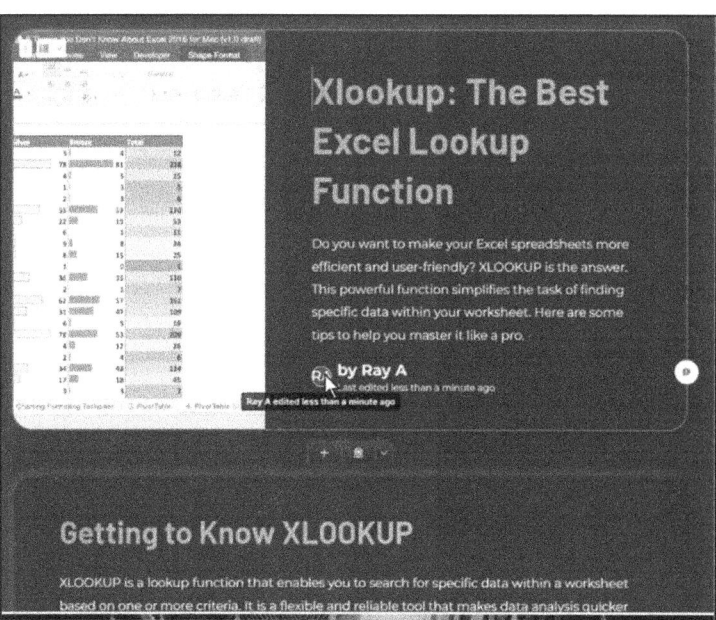

---
[94] https://tome.ai

Implications for L&D: The GenAI tools can help eliminate manual work and swiftly create a draft representation of the presentation slides. The AI engine can design slides based on a specified skeleton of content. It follows a structure, is well-organized, and has all the necessary details. You can force it to use contextual images from a specific repository. In most cases, it provides enough structure to make it easier for instructors to populate relevant information and quickly create engaging presentations.

Step 4: Creating Problem-Solving Case Scenarios

Typical enterprise process: Most jobs now require higher-order problem-solving, technical, troubleshooting, and decision-making skills. L&D professionals greatly emphasize building scenario-based, thinking-intensive content that allows learners to practice on certain expectations. Typically, scenarios are designed based on field events or canned scenarios provided by SMEs. It is a manual process conducted by instructional designers and SMEs, which can be quite time-consuming. However, GenAI tools can help us streamline the effort required and expedite the course development process.

Extending GenAI to achieve this goal: I prompted ChatGPT to create one case study for students to solve:

Prompt <*Create one case study for students to solve. The case study should focus on fixing errors in the XLOOKUP function output. Create the case study in an interesting story format.*>

As shown in Figure 1.6, ChatGPT generated a detailed story-based self-contained case study with necessary variables like situation, problem, constraints, and questions to test learners' deeper understanding and help them troubleshoot common scenarios when using the XLOOKUP function.

Figure 1.6: ChatGPT input and output to create case study assignments

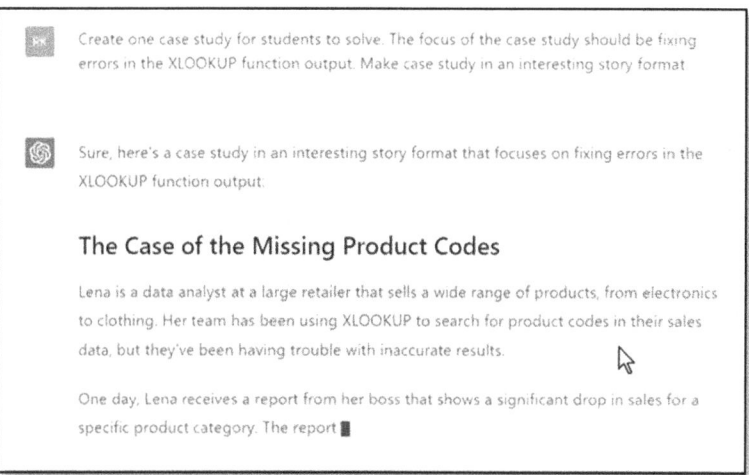

Implications for L&D: Using GenAI tools, you can create powerful case study assignments by instructing the tool to focus on critical aspects of a challenge. You can instruct it to develop a story-based case study for students to solve. Moreover, if relevant materials for developing case study exercises are provided, GenAI can create well-structured case study assignments.

Step 5: Creating Learners' Assessments and Assignments

Typical enterprise process: Most training courses include assessments, quizzes, or exams during and at the end of the training modules. Depending on the job, the nature of the assessment varies. The assessment can be in various formats, such as multiple-choice, short answer, or essay type. Here, you can leverage the power of ChatGPT to build systematic and highly targeted assessments for the training program.

Extending GenAI to achieve this goal: I gave ChatGPT a hypothetical context, stating that the course is targeted for 2 days. I prompted it to suggest and create an appropriate take-home assignment, as shown in Figure 1.7. I also included a prompt for it to create a course-end assessment using the information provided for the course:

Prompt <*What ideal homework should I give the students if the course is spread over two days? Create 2 versions of thinking-intensive homework with challenging assignments. Generate an example of a homework assignment. Generate a 10-question assessment to test students at the end of the course.*>

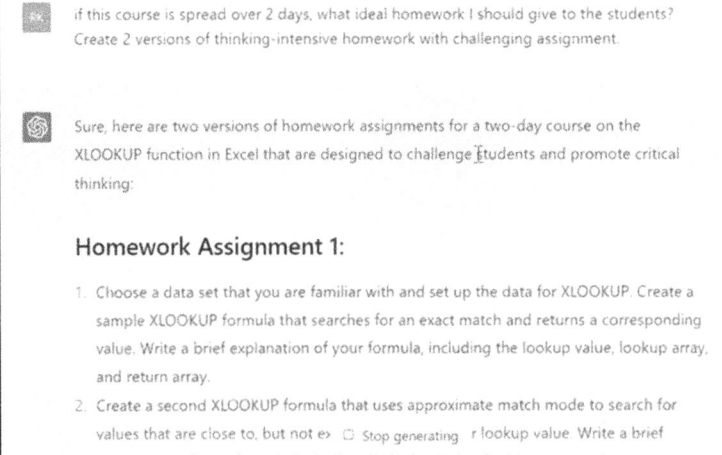

Figure 1.7: ChatGPT input and output to create learners' homework assignments

ChatGPT generated a list of appropriate questions aligned with the scope of the course and level.

Implications for L&D: With appropriate prompts and scoping instructions, GenAI can be customized to provide more challenging assignments. ChatGPT can be used to accelerate the process of creating student assignments and various types of student work and quizzes.

Step 6: Creating Self-learning Content and Videos

Typical enterprise process: More and more training programs are now designed using a blended learning approach. Training material now relies heavily on self-paced content and videos. However, creating self-paced material, especially videos of good quality, is very time-consuming, requiring a range of logistics from cameras, software, editing tools, and other hardware. With GenAI, the content can be created with minimal effort and reduced time.

Extending GenAI to achieve this goal: I used the presentation slide content from Gamma.ai and imported it into another AI tool called PictoryAI[95]. This AI tool converted the presentation slides into a storyboard. It then automatically sequenced all the scenes and video clips contextually. It selects relevant stock footage based on the context and content provided. The enterprise-hosted GenAI tools allow this selection to be contained in corporate repositories only, thus producing highly contextual videos.

---

[95] https://pictory.ai

The created video can be edited for scripts, scenes, clips, and sequences. The video thus created is a faceless video that can be used as online training material.

I thought of making it more attractive in an instructor-style video. Normally, it would have required a considerable setup of greenscreen, cameras, and post-shooting editing, which is a massive investment in cost and time. However, I used another AI tool called D-ID[96], to create a self-learning video in which I used my picture to create a near-realistic replica of myself to narrate the content as a video without having to shoot a single video.

Implications for L&D: Once you add an inbuilt voiceover or the one from your instructor, you can produce a ready-to-deploy, self-paced learning video in no time. Such videos provide learners with a personalized learning experience, sparing them from dispassionate robo-lessons. Some AI tools can intelligently read the transcript and segment or even edit the video into multiple short videos, which can be used appropriately for various learning paths.

Step 7: Deploying GenAI as Trainer

Typical enterprise process: While some organizations have transitioned to remote learning for training, instructor resources are still required to conduct formal training. Instructor resources are the most expensive resources in any training program. However, as you see in the previous step, GenAI has the potential to leverage it to deliver training as a real trainer in the form of self-learning videos or as chatbot, with which learners can have a human-like conversation.

---

[96] https://d-id.com

BONUS 11 / MODELING GEN-AI FOR ENTERPRISE L&D

Extending GenAI to achieve this goal: To demonstrate this, I prompted ChatGPT to act as a trainer and teach me the specified content as if I were a 10-year-old:

Prompt <*I would like you to play the role of trainer. Explain to me how to use the XLOOKUP function with examples. Explain as if I were a 10-year-old. Reply to my follow-up questions, if any. At the end, you should ask me questions to test my understanding.*>

It provided me with a slim-down version of the professional content that was fed into it earlier. As shown in Figure 1.8, it then presented the content in an easy-to-understand manner.

As a learner, I can ask questions, clarify, and expand answers in whatever order I feel is right to understand them thoroughly. Once I provided the context to tone down and simplify the answers for a 10-year-old, it continued to respond with that constraint. For instance, it explained my subsequent queries with examples that are appropriate for a 10-year-old.

Figure 1.8: ChatGPT input and output for using it as a chatbot trainer

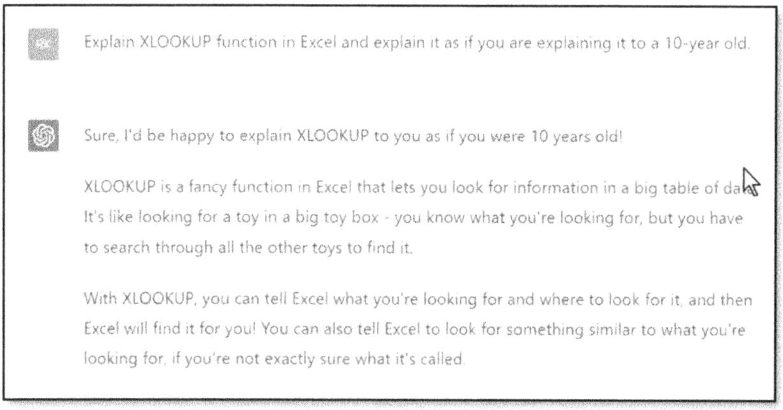

> Explain XLOOKUP function in Excel and explain it as if you are explaining it to a 10-year old.
>
> Sure, I'd be happy to explain XLOOKUP to you as if you were 10 years old!
>
> XLOOKUP is a fancy function in Excel that lets you look for information in a big table of data. It's like looking for a toy in a big toy box - you know what you're looking for, but you have to search through all the other toys to find it.
>
> With XLOOKUP, you can tell Excel what you're looking for and where to look for it, and then Excel will find it for you! You can also tell Excel to look for something similar to what you're looking for, if you're not exactly sure what it's called.

Implications for L&D: GenAI tools can understand the context and provide information specific to users' queries or target audiences. It can be used as a tutor to guide and encourage learners. GenAI can be pre-programmed to ask sense-making questions to adaptively understand a learner's grasp of the topic. This use case holds big promises by combining GenAI, chatbot, adaptive learning paths, and self-learning videos. Using the latest advancements in chatbots, you can engage learners during the learning process in a bidirectional conversation as if each of them has a personalized teacher by their side. Such engaging and lively conversation ultimately facilitates the learning process. In addition, real adaptive learning can happen because GenAI tools will progressively determine the learner's progress and grasp of content and then change the learning path based on the learner's knowledge acquisition level.

Step 8: Deploying GenAI as an Automated Assessor

Typical enterprise process: Assessment of learners is usually a resource-intensive task, regardless of whether you use auto-grading in LMS against a preset answer key or assign an instructor to provide human grading and qualitative feedback. GenAI can make this assessment efficient, deeper, and comprehensive for the assessment questions and feedback.

Extending GenAI to achieve this goal: I prompted ChatGPT to test my understanding of the XLOOKUP function by asking me some questions:

Prompt <*I would like you to test my understanding as a teacher, one question at a time. Check the correctness of my response to each question on a scale of 10, with 10 being the highest. Then give me feedback on what I did wrong.*>

BONUS 11 / MODELING GEN-AI FOR ENTERPRISE L&D

As shown in Figure 1.9, , it asked me questions to test my understanding. It gave me the correct answer with feedback and explained how I could improve my understanding. The interaction is friendly and conversational, like with a tutor. Depending on how well I could engage in a conversation, ChatGPT could go deeper into personalized feedback.

Then, I took it to the next level by assigning ChatGPT the role of an assessor to grade my understanding of XLOOKUP with questions. Not only did it provide instant feedback, but it also graded my responses and suggested the correct answers.

Implications for L&D: GenAI, when implemented as a chatbot with a pre-programmed sequence of questions, can be used to deliver training and assess understanding. Learners will receive in-depth interactive feedback that accurately pinpoints their areas for improvement. It could even offer targeted lessons to close that gap.

Figure 1.9: ChatGPT input and output to act as an adaptive assessor

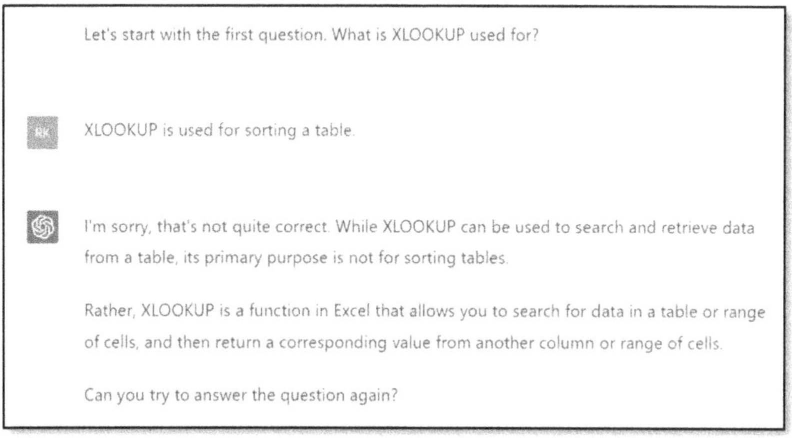

> Let's start with the first question. What is XLOOKUP used for?
>
> XLOOKUP is used for sorting a table.
>
> I'm sorry, that's not quite correct. While XLOOKUP can be used to search and retrieve data from a table, its primary purpose is not for sorting tables.
>
> Rather, XLOOKUP is a function in Excel that allows you to search for data in a table or range of cells, and then return a corresponding value from another column or range of cells.
>
> Can you try to answer the question again?

Step 9: Deploying GenAI as a Support Resource or an Expert Mentor

Typical enterprise process: Training is not a complete solution. Learners also need support in the field, which may come through peer help or expert mentorship. Organizations normally employ performance support systems such as learning portals, communities of practice, and buddy systems. Nevertheless, GenAI has emerged as a great workflow-based performance support system.

Extending GenAI to achieve this goal: To demonstrate this feature, I assigned ChatGPT the role of an expert problem solver. Then, I prompted it for help with an error:

Prompt <*I need expert advice. When I use XLOOKUP in my worksheet, I get #Value error. How do I fix it?*>

Figure 1.10: ChatGPT input and output to act as a support resource

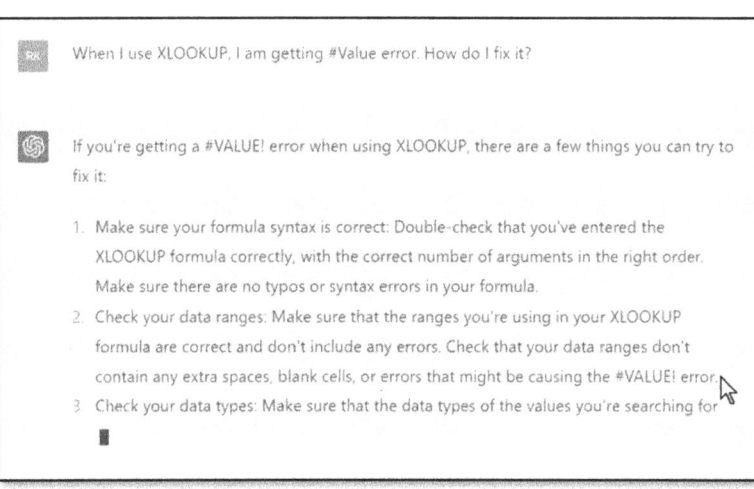

As shown in Figure 1.10, ChatGPT suggested a method to check and correct. If the first suggestion did not work, it provided me with an alternative action plan until the issue was resolved. Thus, ChatGPT served as a helpful buddy or mentor to guide me on-demand during the workflow.

Implications for L&D: If you have new learners who have not received advanced training on specific topics, you can implement a chatbot expert that can be programmed to deliver expert feedback or suggestions in the context of the user's problem. It brings the know-how to the audience's level.

SCALING UP CONSUMER GEN-AI

While most of the steps are invariably used in any standard instructional design project, some of the steps may not be applicable to certain organizations, depending on the nature of the business. However, there is a logical progression of steps to eliminate duplication and minimize efforts in such a way that you could apply the output of the previous step seamlessly into the following step.

Figure 1.11 summarizes the 9 steps demonstrated above as a quick reference. L&D professionals, course designers, and trainers can use this template to conduct their pilots before deciding on full-blown AI implementation.

Figure 1.11: 9 steps to modeling Gen-AI for enterprise L&D applications

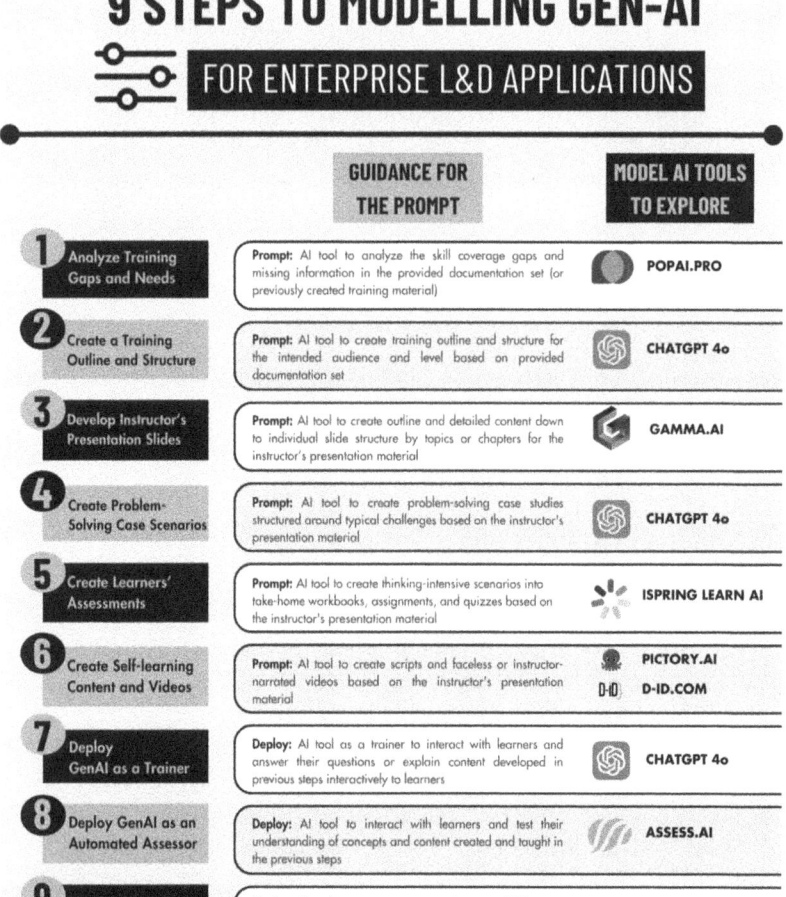

Copyrights © Raman K Attri

BONUS 11 / MODELING GEN-AI FOR ENTERPRISE L&D

GEN-AI FOR ENTERPRISE DOCUMENTATION

Here are additional use cases, not necessarily used in all organizations, that can help L&D specialists or knowledge managers extend GenAI tools into the documentation arena. These use cases may include creating enterprise documentation, developing or extending existing know-how, generating standard operating procedures (SOPs), or even acting as subject matter experts (SMEs). Following are some use cases,

Step 1: Training Custom GenAI Model

Typical enterprise process: SMEs, like engineering departments, develop most standard operating SOPs or procedures within an organization. Generally, these approved SOPs are used in formal training courses to train employees. For GenAI to work for your organization, you must first train the model on these SOPs. Once done, the GenAI model can search, associate, and index that knowledge and learn from it to respond to subsequent queries.

Extending GenAI to achieve this goal: I accomplished that function efficiently through GenAI. I provided ChatGPT with two source documents (custom knowledgebase) on XLOOKUP from two websites (SMEs) from the Internet and prompted it to generate a well-organized procedure:

Prompt < *Refer to two URLs X and Y. You will only use the information from these URLs to respond to subsequent queries. You will not use your pre-trained database. Analyze both procedures and summarize them in clear bullet points.* >

The ChatGPT created its own intelligence based on minimal information it received for given procedures. I asked it to summarize the procedure to validate accuracy (validation).

Implication for L&D: When training on minimal information, Chat GPT can draw conclusions and inferences, giving it the intelligence to process the information and provide valuable insights. Locally hosted GenAI can be trained on organization's documentation and repositories, such as videos, articles, procedures, and PDFs. It may take some time for the model to understand the syntax, organization, and structure of the documents. Once completed, it can create contextual connections to understand the information. GenAI can help organizations improve knowledge generation quickly. Some models can be modeled and trained to learn the mistakes and improve based on user or SME feedback. However, SMEs are responsible for ensuring the accuracy of inputs and outputs generated by the model.

Step 2: Creating Internal SOPs or Procedures

Typical enterprise process: Often, organizations use vendor-supplied procedures as the source and then create contextual procedures for various functions such as design, manufacturing, service, and consumers. Creating such targeted procedures relies on engineering inputs, user reviews, failure reports, and other sources. This becomes a released SOP for that business unit.

Extending GenAI to achieve this goal: I provided ChatGPT with two source documents from the Internet and prompted it to generate a well-organized procedure:

Prompt <*I will provide you with two source documents at two URLs. Read the procedure, make sense of instructions, and create one well-*

organized procedure using only these two procedures. Insert relevant images or tables to illustrate the steps. Use two levels of headings to build the procedures. Present the procedure in a 2-column table with instructions on the left and images or examples on the right.>

It generated a neat, clean, well-structured, tabulated procedure (released SOP).

Implications for L&D: The latest revisions of GenAI tools like ChatGPT can create tables, images, and other kinds of outputs. It can be specifically instructed to use the image or artifacts from the corporate documentation repository. The procedure can be changed in various formats for different applications and also further customized according to user preferences.

Step 3: Creating new SOPs from videos

Typical enterprise process: The corporate knowledge resides in various repositories in various formats, such as presentation slides, documents, PDFs, specifications, spreadsheets, and marketing documents. Video repositories are becoming commonplace. Compiling and converging the knowledge from these incompatible and scattered resources can be highly cumbersome and manual work to create new SOPs. That's where GenAI can come to the rescue.

Extending GenAI to achieve this goal: For this process, I took one of the videos from YouTube on the XLOOKUP function. I used an AI extension to convert the video into a transcript. I fed the transcript to ChatGPT and prompted it to extract useful information and generate a systematic set of instructions based on the video.

Prompt <*I have the following video script of a video available at URL C. I want you to create a new procedure from this information. Do not use any other source or your internal database. Present the procedure in a 2-column table with instructions on the left and images or examples on the right.*>

Implications for L&D: This feature can be handy when converting many videos into instructions or procedures. The latest revisions of GenAI tools like ChatGPT can analyze and work on various inputs like images, videos, audio, documents, schematics, 2D diagrams, and 3D images and output in several different formats. These AI-driven compilations and insights can reduce human efforts significantly and make training development much more efficient.

KEEPING A FEW THINGS IN MIND

You can create all the e-learning content in minutes by integrating various AI tools intelligently and strategically. While validating and refining the content may take some time, the results can be impressive.

GenAI is considered a valuable tool for creating new content in an efficient and contextually relevant manner. While the process of using ChatGPT or other GenAI for L&D projects looks very promising, there are several considerations you need to be aware of in enterprise settings.

Monitor the big picture

Technology has yet to go a long way, though it is rapidly evolving. We are yet to see the full potential of GenAI. Therefore, L&D leaders should exercise caution and look at the complete picture before committing significant investments based on consumer GenAI potential.

Be aware of risks

While all the new AI tools are promising, several unaddressed risks exist, including information security, intellectual property leakage, plagiarism, and liability issues. A key concern among industry professionals is who is responsible for AI-generated content. Such legal implications for AI-generated content are still under discussion. You need to exercise caution before relying heavily on GenAI.

Be sensitive to the impact on jobs

We have yet to see the full social and employment impact of GenAI and other AI tools. A massive shift is occurring where traditional roles such as documentation writers, course developers, e-learning trainers, administrators, and reporters are transitioning into AI versions of those roles. Some of these roles have been automated using AI. Therefore, such an impact on jobs cannot be ignored. As a result, the critical decision would be how far and how fast organizations want to move into GenAI implementation.

Be aware of information and IP security

Lastly, information security is a key concern before L&D leaders can try any pilot program. Everything appears to be on track if you pilot using the Microsoft ecosystem. Microsoft's enterprise version of ChatGPT uses Azure cognitive search to search through millions of documents to index the most relevant information in response to a prompt or question. Microsoft's architecture ensures that all organizational knowledge, documentation, videos, and designs remain within the organization's private knowledge base and are inaccessible to the ChatGPT model.

READERS' LEARNING RESOURCES

Interested readers can access a free, self-paced online course containing 25 videos demonstrating each step described in this article. The course is available at https://get-there-faster.com/enterprise-ai.

Chapter 1
DIGITAL REVOLUTION IN LEARNING TECHNOLOGIES

Chapter 2
BUSINESS KPIs FOR LEARNING TECHNOLOGY

Chapter 3
STRATEGIC LEARNING TECHNOLOGY LEADERSHIP THINKING

Chapter 4
TECHNOLOGIES & ANALYTICS FOR HIRING RIGHT

Chapter 5
TECHNOLOGIES & ANALYTICS FOR PROFICIENCY METRICS

Chapter 6
TECHNOLOGIES & ANALYTICS FOR WORK SKILLS

Chapter 7
TECHNOLOGIES & ANALYTICS FOR EFFICIENT LEARNING PATH

Chapter 8
TECHNOLOGIES & ANALYTICS FOR TIME MEASUREMENTS

Chapter 9
EMERGING TECHNOLOGIES FOR SPEED

Chapter 10
THE FINAL THOUGHTS

BONUS
MODELLING GEN-AI FOR ENTERPRSE L&D

L&D CAREER RESOURCES

L&D CAREER RESOURCES

12/ L&D CAREER RESOURCES

POWER-PACKED L&D BOOKS

Accelerate your learning, training, and technology leadership with the following books. Visit **amazon.com/authors/raman.k.attri** to purchase these books.

Written for training leaders, this book provides a practical and intuitive model for measuring the effectiveness of technical training programs. Through a 4-tier Return on Expectations (ROE) framework, developed through years of research, observation, and experience, this book addresses the challenges in justifying the return on investment (ROI) for large-scale and investment-intensive training programs.

Written for senior e-learning and training leaders who want to shine as CXO executives, this book describes five strategies to institute breakthrough e-learning to shorten TTP. It provides multi-level tips and operational tactics to implement these strategies. You will walk out with an integrated system thinking about a holistic e-learning ecosystem that can shorten TTP metrics.

Written for training designers, this book delivers over 21 training and learning strategies across online learning, classroom instructions, and on-the-job learning that can enable designing workplace training programs to shorten the time-to-proficiency of employees. It provides practical guidance for implementation to equip corporate learning specialists, HR professionals, training leaders, performance consultants, and direct managers.

Written for advanced training designers and strategic learning leaders, this book provides start-to-end methodologies and frameworks to design advanced training programs that prepare workforce with the complex problem-solving skills. This book enables training leaders to stay competitive by developing employees faster to handle unknown, uncertain and unknowable situations faced in an increasingly unpredictable business world.

12/ L&D CAREER RESOURCES

TRAINING COURSES

Accelerate your learning, training, and technology leadership with the following powerful online courses. For more such courses, reach out to Dr Raman K Attri.

Learning Leadership Accelerated

The learning, training, and development space is overcrowded and highly competitive now. Establishing yourself as a distinguished L&D leader is not easy anymore. You need to adopt a specific thought process and proven strategies to speed up your path to becoming a top L&D leader with unique specialization, positioning, and credibility. In this online course, learn the science of accelerating the path to becoming a top-notch learning and training leader. Master strategies, methods, and frameworks to put yourself onto the world map at an accelerated rate.

e-learning Design to Speed Up Learning

Do you need to design online/e-learning courses to speed up the skill acquisition of your learners? But you don't know where to start? The life-changing skills are delivered when you design online or e-learning courses systematically using instructional design practices with the latest and greatest strategies. This training course will teach you a new framework for your e-learning training design. You will walk out with proven, practical e-learning training design strategies from research used by some of the most advanced training organizations across the world. You will learn 3 key elements of e-learning design that you just pay attention to. You will also learn 5 strategies to make your courses powerful. You will adopt a new viewpoint of implementing 5 guiding principles in your e-learning or online courses.

STRATEGIC LEARNING TECHNOLOGY LEADERSHIP

Strategize Technologies to Speed Up Employee Development

The speed with which teams are developed is far more critical now to meet the challenges of complex next-generation projects amidst a fast-paced business environment. Technologies are now the first line of defense to impact how employees learn, develop, and perform at the workplace. In this revolutionary course, you will receive firsthand research-based wisdom on an integrated system thinking on measuring, tracking, and reducing time-to-proficiency using analytics strategically. You will acquire a renewed business acumen by marrying two things—workforce analytics and time-to-proficiency metrics- to build a people analytics strategy that can ensure faster improvement of employee performance. You will learn how futuristic thinking organizations have leveraged state-of-the-art technologies, analytics, tools, and systems to shorten the time-to-proficiency of their workforce and teams at the speed of business.

SCIENCE OF SPEED IN L&D

Supercharge your learning leadership career to new heights by getting certified through a master certification program. For more information, reach out to Dr Raman K Attri.

Chief Learning Officer: Speed-Savvy Learning Leader

Designed for learning and training specialists, training managers, L&D professionals, human resources executives, and coaches to help them shine as world-class, speed-savvy learning thought leaders. The certification is awarded through rigorous training and qualification to develop the participants as the world's top-notch experts on accelerated learning in organizational space. Based on two decades of research, experience, experimentation, and authoring, this certification is structured around 5 power-packed tracks to qualify ambitious learning specialists who want to master the science of speed in learning, training, performance, and employee development.

Chief Training Design Guru: Speed-Savvy Training Designer

Designed for learning and training specialists, training professionals, trainers, instructional designers, speakers, coaches, and teachers, to help them shine as highly sought-after training design strategists. This certification is awarded through rigorous training and qualification to develop the participants as the world's top-notch experts in designing complex training and mentoring programs. If you need to equip your learners and audience with complex skills and improve their performance faster, then this advanced certification is for you. Based on two decades of research, experience, experimentations, and authoring, this certification is structured around 5 power-packed tracks to teach you the breakthrough, advanced, integrated methodologies for start-to-end analysis, design, development, and delivery of your training programs. Take your learning design to the next level by mastering the design of transformational coaching, mentoring, and certification programs.

BIBLIOGRAPHY

FOOTNOTES (in the order of appearance)

1. 10 eLearning Software Trends for 2022/2023. https://financesonline.com/elearning-software-trends/
2. Thinkific, https://www.thinkific.com/elearning-trends/
3. ActivTrack. Employee Monitor Software. https://www.activtrak.com/solutions/employee-monitoring/
4. Bock, L. (2015). Work Rules!: Insights from Inside Google That Will Transform How You Live and Lead. Hachette Books.
5. Estrada-Cedeno et. al. 2019. The Good, the Bad and the Ugly: Workers Profiling through Clustering Analysis. https://www.researchgate.net/publication/332291665
6. Gomes C et. Al. 2015. Better Off together: A cluster analysis of self-leadership and its relationship to individual innovation in hospital nurses. Psicologia. Vol. 29 (1), 45-58. https://core.ac.uk/download/pdf/302955271.pdf
7. Salesforce Corp, https://www.salesforce.com/products/analytics/overview/?d=cta-body-promo-32
8. Tableau, https://www.tableau.com/
9. Microsoft Corp, https://powerbi.com
10. IBM (n.d.), Job Master. https://www.ibm.com/case-studies/jobmaster-talent-solutions-recruitment-assessment
11. RapidMiner. https://rapidminer.com/
12. Smith, J., & Jones, M. (2022). The impact of employee training on job performance: A regression analysis. Journal of Workplace Learning, 34(1), 45-60.

BIBLIOGRAPHY

13. Deloitte. 2018 Global Human Capital Trends. https://www2.deloitte.com/content/dam/Deloitte/uk/Documents/human-capital/deloitte-uk-human-capital-trends-2018.pdf
14. JANZZ Technology. https://janzz.technology/
15. Ideal. S&P Data increased retention by 20%. https://ideal.com/customer/sp-data/
16. Karp, A. (n.d.). HiredScore. The Rise of Talent Intelligence. Talent Tech Labs. https://www.hiredscore.com/resources?type=Case+Studies
17. https://www.hirevue.com/
18. Modern Hire. Assessing Candidates for Call Center Customer Service Roles. https://modernhire.com/call-center-customer-service/
19. Albinus, P. (2021). How Chevron Drilled into Its HR Data to Tap New Talent. https://hrexecutive.com/how-chevron-drilled-into-its-hr-data-to-tap-new-talent/
20. Maier S. (2016). How Google Uses People Analytics to Create a Great Workplace. Entreprenuer. https://www.entrepreneur.com/growing-a-business/how-google-uses-people-analytics-to-create-a-great-workplace/284550
21. https://www.ciosummits.com/media/solution_spotlight/106462_0713.pdf
22. Breschi, R., Carlin, D., & Schaininger, B. (2018). Matching the right talent to the right roles. https://www.mckinsey.com/capabilities/people-and-organizational-performance/our-insights/the-organization-blog/matching-the-right-talent-to-the-right-roles
23. Garvin, D. A. (2013). How Google Sold Its Engineers on Management. Harvard Business Review. Retrieved from https://hbr.org/2013/12/how-google-sold-its-engineers-on-management
24. Visier. Why Employee Skills Must Be Measured. https://www.visier.com/blog/why-employee-skills-must-be-measured/
25. https://www.linkedin.com/pulse/workforce-analytics-journey-jp-morgan-chase-david-green
26. https://www.teramind.co/
27. https://clockify.me/
28. https://www.intlock.com/blog/microsoft-workplace-analytics/
29. RealWear, https://www.realwear.com/field-services/
30. Microsoft Corp, https://www.microsoft.com/en-us/hololens/hardware
31. Meta Corp, https://www.meta.com/quest/products/quest-2/
32. https://www.scopear.com/
33. https://www.medicalrealities.com/technology

BIBLIOGRAPHY

34. https://www.mondly.com/vr
35. https://nearpod.com/nearpod-vr
36. https://yousician.com/lp/yousician
37. IBM Corp, https://www.ibm.com/cloud/watson-studio
38. https://www.tibco.com/products/tibco-spotfire
39. SAP Corp, https://www.sap.com/products/technology-platform/lumira.html
40. https://www.qlik.com/us/
41. Microsoft Corp, https://powerbi.microsoft.com/en-us/
42. ChatGPT, https://chat.openai.com/
43. Microsoft Corp, https://www.microsoft.com/en-us/microsoft-copilot
44. Gemini AI tool, https://gemini.google.com/app
45. IBM Corp, https://www.ibm.com/products/watson-assistant
46. https://you.com/
47. Perplexity AI tool, https://perplexity.ai/
48. https://www.algolia.com/products/ai-search
49. Arnold, V., P. Collier, S. Leech, S. Sutton, and A. Vincent, 2013, INCASE: Simulating experience to accelerate expertise development by knowledge workers, International Journal of Intelligent Systems in Accounting, Finance and Management 20, 1–21.
50. https://www.knowledgeowl.com/features/
51. https://www.screensteps.com/
52. https://www.userlane.com/platform/context-sensitive-help/
53. https://powerautomate.microsoft.com/en-us/
54. https://onscreen.us/onscreen-for-web-apps/
55. IBM Connections Engagement Suite offers an integrated set of solutions for increasing employee engagement, collaboration, and productivity. https://www.ibm.com/common/ssi/ShowDoc.wss?docURL=/common/ssi/rep_ca/5/897/ENUS217-535/index.html&lang=en&request_locale=en
56. Garfield, S. 2021. Expertise Locators and Ask the Expert. https://lucidea.com/blog/km-component-35-expertise-locators-and-ask-the-expert/
57. Microsoft Corp, https://www.microsoft.com/en-us/microsoft-365/yammer/yammer-overview
58. https://www.jivesoftware.com/
59. Slack, https://slack.com/

BIBLIOGRAPHY

60. https://www.atlassian.com/software/confluence
61. Microsoft Corp, https://www.microsoft.com/en-ww/microsoft-teams/teams-for-work
62. https://www.twilio.com/
63. HubSpot, https://www.hubspot.com/
64. SalesForce, https://www.salesforce.com/
65. Slack, https://slack.com/
66. Murtaza et al. 2022. AI-based personalized e-learning systems: Issues, Challenges, and Solutions. Vol 10. 81323-81242. https://ieeexplore.ieee.org/document/9840390/
67. https://www.duolingo.com/
68. Learndash. 2020. 4 examples of Ai being Used In E-learning. https://www.learndash.com/4-examples-of-ai-being-used-in-e-learning/
69. Michelle, E. 2023. Use of AI in eLearning. https://elearningindustry.com/use-of-ai-in-elearning
70. https://colorwhistle.com/impact-of-ai-in-elearning-industry/
71. Intel Corp, https://www.intel.com/content/dam/www/central-libraries/us/en/documents/2023-10/ai-in-education-whitepaper.pdf
72. Khan Academy, https://blog.khanacademy.org/new-khanmigo-interests/
73. ChatGPT from OpenAI, https://chat.openai.com
74. Gemini AI from Google, https://gemini.google.com
75. Microsoft Co-pilot AI, https://copilot.microsoft.com
76. Cloude AI, https://claude.ai
77. eLearning Industry (2023, Aug 17). The Role Of Artificial Intelligence In Instructional Design. https://elearningindustry.com/role-of-artificial-intelligence-in-instructional-design
78. Future1st (2023, June 18). *How to Create a Structured Training Program for Your Trainees.* https://www.future1st.com.au/post/how-to-create-a-structured-training-program-for-your-trainees
79. Hylenski, P (2024). Revolutionizing Training with AI-Created Videos, LinkedIn newsletter, https://www.linkedin.com/pulse/revolutionizing-training-ai-created-videos-paul-hylenski-jaeve/
80. Forbes (2024, Feb). Revolutionizing Business Decision-Making: The Impact Of Generative AI On Predictive Analytics. https://www.forbes.com/sites/forbestechcouncil/2024/02/23/revolutionizing-business-decision-making-the-impact-of-generative-ai-on-predictive-analytics/

BIBLIOGRAPHY

81. Gad-Elrab, A. A. (2021). Modern business intelligence: Big data analytics and artificial intelligence for creating the data-driven value. In E-Business-Higher Education and Intelligence Applications, Wu, R & Mircea, M (eds.), 135, Intech Open, https://www.intechopen.com/chapters/76332

82. NVIDIA Omniverse (2023, Sep). How AI-Generated 3D Models are Transforming 3D Pipelines. https://medium.com/@nvidiaomniverse/how-ai-generated-3d-models-are-transforming-3d-pipelines-d4245566a289

83. FxM web (2024, Feb). AI's Pioneering Role: Navigating the Metaverse, VR, and AR Realms. https://www.fxmweb.com/insights/ai-s-pioneering-role-navigating-the-metaverse-vr-and-ar-realms.html

84. Camola, V., Bansal, G., et al. (2023, July 28). Beyond Reality: The Pivotal Role of Generative AI in the Metaverse - arXiv. https://arxiv.org/abs/2308.06272

85. Rasheed, Z., Ghwanmeh, S., & Abualkishik, A. Z. (2023). Harnessing Artificial Intelligence for Personalized Learning: A Systematic Review. Data and Metadata. 2,146. https://doi.org/10.56294/dm2023146

86. ChatDoc AI tool, https://chatdoc.ai

87. Humat AI tool, https://humata.ai

88. PopAI tool, https://popai.pro

89. MindGrasp AI tool, https://mindgrasp.ai

90. ChatDoc AI tool, https://chatdoc.ai

91. Ask Viable AI tool, https://askviable.com

92. DocLime AI tool, https://doclime.com

93. Gamm AI tool, https://gamma.ai

94. Tome AI tool, https://tome.ai

95. Pictory AI tool, https://pictory.ai

96. D-iD AI tool, https://d-id.com

ADDITIONAL REFERENCES

Appian (2024). Expert Advice on Navigating the AI Economy. *2024 AI Outlook report.* https://appian.com/learn/resources/resource-center/google/2023/2024-ai-outlook

Kaur, J., & Kumar, V. (2013). Competency mapping: A gap Analysis. *International Journal of Education and Research*, 1(1), 1-9.

Olufayo, B. A., & Akinbo, T. M. (2021). Training gap identification as determinant of employees' job performance in gas and energy company in delta state,

BIBLIOGRAPHY

Nigeria. *Journal of Human Resource Management*, 9(4), 108-119. doi: 10.11648/j.jhrm.20210904.13

Future1st (2023, June 18). *How to Create a Structured Training Program for Your Trainees*. https://www.future1st.com.au/post/how-to-create-a-structured-training-program-for-your-trainees

Mode-Cater, O. & Cole, L. (2023, June 26). Crafting Compelling Training Presentations for Employees, *Training Magazine online*. https://trainingmag.com/crafting-compelling-training-presentations-for-employees/

Oser, R. L., Gualtieri, J. W., Cannon-Bowers, J. A., & Salas, E. (1999). Training Team Problem Solving Skills: An Event-based Approach. *Computers in human behavior*, 15(3-4), 441-462. doi: 10.1016/S0747-5632(99)00031-X

Kirschner, P., Carr, C., Van Merriënboer, J., & Sloep, P. (2002). How expert designers design. *Performance Improvement Quarterly*, 15(4), 86-104. doi: 10.1111/j.1937-8327.2002.tb00267.x

El-Ariss, B., Zaneldin, E., & Ahmed, W. (2021). Using videos in blended e-learning for a structural steel design course. *Education Sciences*, 11(6), 290. doi: 10.3390/educsci11060290

TrainerBubble (2024, Feb 5). *Does Instructor-Led Training Still Have a Place in Corporate Learning?* https://www.trainerbubble.com/does-instructor-led-training-still-have-a-place-in-corporate-learning/

Sargent, R. (2017). *Gamifying self-assessments in online corporate training: Points and levels* (Doctoral dissertation, Northcentral University). https://www.proquest.com/openview/bb1c2c95e110f70ec2e927b9550934e8/

Vleetech (2024, Feb 22). *Generative AI Risks and Regulatory Issues*. https://www.velvetech.com/blog/generative-ai-risks-regulations/

Juarez, S. & Cavanagh, L. (2023, May 1). *Making Enterprise GPT Real with Azure Cognitive Search and Azure OpenAI service*, AI Show (Microsoft). https://learn.microsoft.com/en-us/shows/ai-show/making-enterprise-gpt-real-with-azure-cognitive-search-and-azure-openai-service

RECOMMENDED READINGS

Donald H Taylor, Learning Technologies in the Workplace: How to Successfully Implement Learning Technologies in Organizations, 2017, Kogan Page.

Donald Clark, Learning Technology: A Complete Guide for Learning Professionals, 2013, Kogan Page.

BIBLIOGRAPHY

Nick Rushby, Dan Surry (Editors), the Wiley Handbook of Learning Technology, 2016, Wiley.

Stacey Harris, Introduction to HR Technologies: Understand How to Use Technology to Improve Performance and Processes, 2021, Kogan.

Donald Clark, Artificial Intelligence for Learning: How to Use AI to Support Employee Development, 2020, Kogan Page.

Elias Carayannis, Strategic Management of Technological Learning, 2000, CRC Press.

INDEX

A

ability 6, 19, 47, 54, 55, 57, 82, 90, 91, 112, 136, 163, 182, 187, 221
    ability to assess 82
    ability to compete 54, 55
    ability to increase 55
    ability to multitask 90
    ability to produce 112
    ability to provide 182
    ability to read 221
    ability to reinforce 187
academic 8, 10, 217
    academic credentials 10
    academic integrity 8
    academic magazine 217
accelerate 26, 34, 36, 37, 40, 48, 49, 54, 84, 91, 145, 170, 185, 187, 189, 197, 199, 207–9, 212, 231
    accelerate development 207, 209
    accelerate employee learning 40
    accelerate employee skill 54
    accelerate expertise 185
    accelerate expertise development
    accelerate learning 199
    accelerate proficiency 170, 187
    accelerate the speed-to-proficiency 36
    accelerate TTP 37
accelerating 21, 32, 37, 52, 53, 207, 219
    accelerating employee learning 53
    accelerating employee skill 53
    accelerating employee skill acquisition 53
    accelerating skill acquisition 52
    accelerating software development 52
    accelerating technological changes 21
    accelerating the expertise 32
accessible 3, 5, 6, 9, 11, 159, 167, 169, 171, 186, 201
    accessible technologies 159
accomplishment 48, 194, 209
    accomplishment-based 194
achievement 48, 92, 101, 102, 136, 137, 164, 209
    achievement of proficiency 102
acquire 22, 24, 34, 35, 50, 72, 75, 135
    acquire complex skills 34
    acquire new skills 22, 50, 135
    acquire next-generation skills 24
acquisition 52–54, 161, 234
adaptive 6, 7, 19, 52, 131, 133, 135, 137, 138, 168, 169, 201, 234, 235
    adaptive assessor 235

INDEX

adaptive learning 6, 19, 52, 135, 137, 168, 201, 234
adaptive learning opportunities 201
adaptive learning paths 135, 168, 234
adaptive learning platforms 52
adaptive learning systems 137
adaptive learning technologies 6, 135
adaptive LMS 168
adaptive mentoring 137
adaptive paths 168
adaptive systems 137, 168, 169
adaptive technologies 138
advanced 54, 86, 87, 120, 124, 168, 175, 225, 237
   advanced algorithm 168
   advanced analysis 124
   advanced analytics 87
   advanced data 86
   advanced methods 175
   advanced skill 120
   advanced technologies 54
   advanced training 237
advancements 3, 6, 13, 234
AI (see: artificial intelligence)
AI-based 89, 124, 136, 152, 159, 160, 180, 182, 198–201
   AI-based e-learning 198, 201
   AI-based learning 136, 200
   AI-based learning systems 136
   AI-based personalized e-learning
   AI-based personalized learning 199
   AI-based platforms 201
   AI-based practice 200
   AI-based resources 201
   AI-based search engines 180, 182
   AI-based skill analysis 124
   AI-based systems 124, 136
   AI-based technologies 89, 152, 159, 160

AI-based tutors 201
AI-based workforce analytics 124
AI-created
AI-driven 180, 201, 218, 219, 242
   AI-driven course 218
   AI-driven data 180
   AI-driven instructional design 219
   AI-driven instructional material 218
   AI-driven solutions 201
   AI-driven training 218
AI-generated 243
   AI-generated 3D models
   AI-generated content 243
AI-personalized learning 218
AI-powered 9, 85, 89, 169
   AI-powered algorithm 89
   AI-powered tools 9
algorithmic 133, 136, 138
   algorithmic LMS systems 136
algorithms 6, 92, 93, 135, 168, 177, 199
analytics 3, 6, 21, 22, 25, 51, 54–56, 64, 67–71, 75, 81, 83–91, 93–95, 101, 102, 105, 106, 109–11, 119–22, 124, 125, 131, 133, 135–38, 145–52, 159–67, 170, 176, 180, 181, 218, 221
   analytics across business units 54
   analytics for performer profiling 167
   analytics for proficiency metrics 167
   analytics for TTP measurements 149
   analytics for work skills 167
   analytics on employee activities 83
   analytics on event frequency 121
   analytics on measuring time-to-productivity 166
   analytics platform 86

INDEX

analytics to manage talent 161
analytics to track time 149
analyze 19, 21, 25, 70, 72, 85–92,
    110, 111, 119, 123–25, 131, 136,
    145, 146, 162, 165, 181, 199,
    200, 219, 221, 222, 239, 242
  analyze candidates 90
  analyze content gaps 222
  analyze data 91, 136, 146, 181
  analyze employee performance 87
  analyze employee skills 111, 124
  analyze learner behavior 21
  analyze sales data 123
  analyze student data 199
  analyze the patterns 145
  analyze the sequences 131
  analyze the work 119, 125
  analyze time variables 145
  analyze workforce data 92
application 3, 4, 19, 123, 146, 167,
    169, 171, 172, 177, 181–83, 188,
    189, 197, 200, 217, 218, 238, 241
  application interface 188
AR (see: augmented reality)
AR-based 134, 180, 184
  AR-based job 180
  AR-based job instructions 180
  AR-based PSSs 184
  AR-based technologies 134
artificial intelligence 7, 217–19
assessment 3, 4, 6, 8, 10, 75, 84, 90,
    91, 108, 110, 112, 120, 159, 164,
    165, 169, 170, 173, 197, 199,
    217, 219, 220, 223, 229, 230, 234
  assessment data 120
  assessment mechanism 112
  assessment platform 90
  assessment questions 234
  assessment technologies 170
  assessment tools 4
assessment-driven 111
  assessment-driven proficiency 111

assessment-driven technologies
    111
assignment 111, 133, 134, 136, 137,
    229–31
augmentation 178, 218
augmented 6, 171, 172, 184, 189
  augmented displays 172
  augmented headset 184
  augmented reality 6
auto-grading 234
automation 23, 37, 124, 133, 159
  automation through technologies
    133

B

baseline 28, 55, 64–66, 111, 112, 151
  baseline time-to-proficiency 65
  baseline TTP 64, 66
benchmark 30, 101, 151
blended learning 8, 231
blockchain 9, 10
  blockchain technology 9, 10
business 20, 21, 24, 26, 31, 33–39,
    50, 51, 54, 55, 57, 62, 64, 65, 72,
    74, 75, 83, 85, 86, 92, 93, 95,
    101–3, 105–7, 109–11, 120, 121,
    123, 150, 161, 162, 165, 166,
    181, 182, 186, 195, 198, 218,
    237, 240
  business administration 110
  business benefits 38, 102
  business case 35
  business challenge 37
  business conditions 101
  business consultants 38
  business context 102
  business continuity 20
  business corporations 186
  business decision-making
  business drivers 31, 33, 35, 36
  business environment 51, 55
  business executives 74

INDEX

business gains 38
business goals 105
business intelligence 121, 123, 218
business KPIs 57, 165
business metrics 37, 39, 102
business needs 50, 51, 95
business objectives 92, 111
business operations 62, 166
business outcomes 26, 37, 57, 93, 105–7, 120, 150, 162
business performance 26, 162
business pressures 34
business procedures 186
business processes 195
business results 64, 107, 109, 110
business strategy 75, 103
business success 85, 161
business units 20, 54, 166

C

capability 21, 22, 35, 36, 83, 90, 92, 94, 148, 181, 182, 187, 189, 207, 208, 217
capital-intensive 19, 22, 73
   capital-intensive learning technologies 22
certification 3, 84, 122, 159, 165, 166
   certification, compliance 3
   certification program 122
chatbot 9, 180, 182, 183, 200, 232–35, 237
   chatbot expert 237
   chatbot trainer 233
ChatGPT 198, 217–20, 223–31, 233–37, 239–43
   ChatGPT 4.0 plugins 227
   ChatGPT created 240
   ChatGPT generated 226, 228, 231
   ChatGPT-generated 226

ChatGPT input 224, 226, 229, 230, 233, 235, 236
ChatGPT model 220, 243
ChatGPT output 224
cloud-based 180, 181, 193
   cloud-based applications 181
   cloud-based data analysis 180
   cloud-based databases 193
   cloud-based data sources 181
   cloud-based document editing 193
coaching 3, 25, 48, 58, 159, 164, 169, 170, 178, 189, 218
   coaching platforms 170
   coaching processes 58
   coaching stage 164
   coaching technologies 170
   coaching tools 159
collaboration 4, 12, 48, 52, 191–94, 196
   collaboration functions 194
   collaboration platforms 191, 196
   collaboration skills 12
   collaboration technologies 192, 193
   collaboration tools 48, 52, 192, 193
competencies 67, 72, 81, 84, 137, 220
competency-based 6
competitiveness 13, 31–34, 37, 38
competitors 20, 23, 51, 54
concept 5, 6, 9, 55
connectivity 135, 194, 196, 207–9
consistent 30, 31, 105, 147, 183
content 8, 70, 83, 89, 119, 124, 131, 135–37, 159, 169–71, 177, 180, 186–89, 195, 199–201, 217–23, 226–28, 231–34, 242, 243
   content-based 217
   content-driven 225
   content-focused 169
   content-heavy 187
context-based 182

INDEX

context-sensitive 188
contextual 180, 184, 187–89, 228, 231, 240
   contextual connections 240
   contextual help 187–89
   contextual images 228
   contextual instructions 184
   contextual procedures 240
   contextual videos 231
corporation 9, 92, 174, 186
cost-effectiveness 23
cost-efficiency 35, 36
CRM (see: customer relationship management)
customer 31, 33–35, 38, 54, 57, 65, 85–87, 89–91, 103–7, 109, 110, 165, 166, 182, 183, 185, 187, 194, 198
   customer calls 103, 104, 166
   customer engagement 86
   customer expectations 35
   customer experience 183, 185
   customer feedback 86
   customer issues 182
   customer needs 38
   customer pressures 33
   customer relationship 86, 109
   customer relationship management 86, 109
   customer satisfaction 38, 85, 87, 91, 103–5, 107, 165
   customer satisfaction improvement 38
   customer satisfaction score 91, 103, 104, 107, 165
customer service 31, 54, 57, 86, 90, 91, 106, 185, 198
   customer service executives 106
   customer service helpdesk 31
   customer service metrics 54
   customer service representatives 86
   customer service roles 90
   customer service skills 91
   customer service speed 54

D

dashboards 147, 150, 151, 181
decision-maker 48, 49, 147, 208, 209
decision-making 9, 49, 177, 186, 187, 218, 228
decisions 25, 49, 75, 91, 93, 95, 123, 124, 162, 180, 181
decision-support 134, 180, 181, 185
   decision-support software 134, 180, 181, 185
   decision-support systems 180, 181
decision-tree 87, 169
designed 5, 52–54, 58, 62, 120, 122, 131, 146, 185, 188, 189, 198, 228, 231
development 4–6, 8, 11, 19–21, 23–25, 27, 31, 37, 40, 47–55, 57, 59, 62, 65, 66, 68, 71, 72, 75, 86, 124, 138, 152, 161, 162, 166–69, 185, 199, 200, 207, 209, 217, 219, 220, 222, 228, 242
   development journey 25, 27, 54, 166, 168
digital 9, 10, 12, 13, 21, 40, 64, 172–74
   digital age 21
   digital communities 12
   digital elements 174
   digital environment 173
   digital information 172
   digital learning trends 12
   digital ledger 10
   digital revolution 13, 40
   digital transformation 64
disruptions 7
document 180, 185, 187, 188, 193, 201, 221, 239–43
documentation 3, 4, 182, 183, 188, 189, 222, 223, 239–41, 243

INDEX

documentation repositories 183

E

ecosystem 24, 55–57, 59, 63, 64, 88, 178, 212, 243
e-learning 3–5, 7–12, 73–75, 185, 198–201, 218, 242, 243
   e-learning content 242
   e-learning industry 8, 9
   e-learning platforms 12, 74, 199–201
   e-learning resources 185
   e-learning solutions 201
   e-learning strategy 75
   e-learning systems 185, 200
   e-learning technologies 74
   e-learning tools 4, 8, 198
   e-learning trainers 243
employee 3, 19–25, 27, 29–31, 33, 36, 37, 40, 47–55, 57, 58, 62, 65–68, 71, 72, 75, 81, 83–90, 92–94, 101, 104, 109–11, 121, 123–25, 132, 133, 135, 137, 138, 146, 147, 150, 152, 163, 165–70, 177, 181, 184, 186, 187, 189, 192, 196
   employee abilities 57
   employee activities 83, 84
   employee analytics 89, 90, 124
   employee behavior 83, 124
   employee competitiveness 31
   employee data 52, 54, 81, 86, 87, 111
   employee development 20, 23–25, 27, 37, 40, 47, 48, 50–55, 57, 62, 65, 66, 68, 71, 72, 75, 152, 166–69
   employee engagement 19, 50, 89
   employee experiences 132
   employee monitoring 146
   employee onboarding 184
   employee performance 29, 49, 55, 57, 67, 84, 85, 87, 88, 101, 110, 123, 137, 167, 181
   employee productivity 85, 87, 150
   employee proficiency 54, 68, 101, 111, 121, 163
   employee profile 92
   employee profiling (see: employee - employee profile)
   employee satisfaction 94
   employee skills 111, 124
   employee success 87
   employee turnover 50, 147
employee retention 22, 92, 93, 125
engagement 11, 19, 50, 84, 86, 89, 110, 112, 146, 165, 172, 176, 192, 201
   engagement levels 146
   engagement metrics 165
enterprise 191, 194, 198, 199, 215, 218–20, 222, 225, 228, 229, 231, 232, 234, 236, 238–43
   enterprise AI 219
   enterprise devices 191
   enterprise documentation 239
   enterprise learning 218, 219
   enterprise process 220, 222, 225, 228, 229, 231, 232, 234, 236, 239–41
   enterprise settings 242
   enterprise systems 198
environment 4, 6, 8, 9, 11–13, 35, 51, 52, 55, 57–61, 106, 134, 173, 184, 196
   environment support 58, 60
   environment support systems 58, 60
   environment technologies 61
equipment 11, 121, 124, 172, 173, 184, 189
   equipment company 121
   equipment repair 189
experience-building 31

INDEX

experiences 4–6, 9, 11, 13, 48, 132, 135, 136, 169, 172, 174, 175, 183, 194, 200, 201
expertise 30, 32, 83, 84, 185, 189, 193–95
  expertise databases 194
  expertise locator 194, 195
  expertise taxonomy 194
expertise development

F

feedback 5, 9, 10, 12, 48, 49, 52, 82, 86, 137, 146, 174–76, 189, 192, 200, 201, 221, 234, 235, 237, 240
  feedback systems 52, 82
first-time-right 103
  first-time-right resolution 103

G

gadgets 133, 173, 183
game-based 112
  game-based learning 112
  game-based learning platform 112
game-like features 174
games 5, 176
gamification 5, 168, 171, 174–76
  gamification elements 5, 175
  gamification technologies 5, 168
gamified 11, 112, 173–75
  gamified assessments 112
  gamified homework 112
  gamified learning 173
  gamified virtual immersive technologies 11
  gamified virtual world 174
gaming 134, 172–74, 176
  gaming environments 134
  gaming scenarios 174
gen-AI 215, 217–23, 225, 228–36, 238–43

gen-AI for enterprise L&D 215, 238
generative AI 218
Google 85, 93, 94, 111, 168, 172, 182, 193, 217

H

hands-free 184
  hands-free headsets 184
hands-on 9, 11, 186, 201, 223
  hands-on activities 223
  hands-on learning 201
  hands-on learning experiences 201
  hands-on skills 186
healthcare 9, 32, 48, 52, 91, 94
higher-order 20, 228
  higher-order problem-solving 228
  higher-order strategic thinking 20
high-performing 85, 111
  high-performing managers 111
hiring 27, 34, 35, 62, 63, 67, 75, 81–85, 87–95, 162, 163, 211
  hiring decisions 91, 93
  hiring managers 92
  hiring practices 95
  hiring process 88, 89, 91, 93
  hiring profile 83, 84
  hiring stage 81, 163
hiring-focused 83
Hololens 9, 134, 172
hyper-realistic 217

I

ILT (see: instructor-led)
immersive 6, 9, 11, 13, 134, 168, 172–76
  immersive environment 11
  immersive experience 13, 134, 172–74, 176

INDEX

immersive gaming 134
immersive learning 6, 9, 11, 175
immersive models 172
immersive storylines 176
immersive technologies 11, 175
immersive VR 9
implementation 19, 20, 23–25, 40, 47, 49, 53, 70, 75, 193, 194, 207, 212, 237, 243
implication 33, 34, 221, 225, 228, 229, 231, 232, 234, 235, 237, 240–43
improvement targets 151
individual 6, 10, 29, 30, 48, 67, 86, 132, 138, 145, 147, 149, 151
  individual activity 132
  individual employees 138
  individual functions 149
  individual innovation 86
  individual learners 6
  individual learning 10
  individual needs 48
individualized 187
  individualized online access 187
informal 29, 196
  informal learning 29, 196
  informal training (see: informal - informal learning)
information 84, 86, 92, 124, 136, 145, 168–72, 176–78, 182, 184, 185, 187, 188, 195, 221, 223, 228, 230, 234, 239–43
informational 186, 187
informational content 186, 187
innovation 20, 47, 86, 176
insights 21, 84–86, 89, 90, 93, 101, 136, 146, 161, 162, 180, 181, 183, 200, 218, 240, 242
instructional 217–19, 225, 226, 228, 237
  instructional design 217–19, 237
  instructional designer 225, 226, 228

instructional design processes 217
instructional design project 237
instructional material 218
instructional material development 218
instructions 172, 173, 180, 184, 188, 227, 231, 240–42
instructor 4, 176, 185, 226, 228, 232, 234
instructor-led 8, 135, 169, 186, 187, 225
  instructor-led event 135
  instructor-led session 186
  instructor-led training 135, 169, 187
  instructor-led videos 225
interactions (see: interactive)
interactive 3–5, 9, 11, 135, 159, 171, 175, 181, 184, 188, 192, 196, 197, 207, 209, 235
  interactive feedback 235
  interactive guides 188
  interactive leaderboards 175
  interactive learning 9, 11, 135
  interactive learning opportunities 11
  interactive videos 171
  interactive virtual classrooms 11
  interactive visualizations 181
intervention 25, 27, 39, 62, 185–87, 222
investment 22, 73, 74, 94, 106, 162, 232, 243

J

JIT (see: just-in-time)
job-fit 93, 94
jobs 26, 31, 33, 35, 94, 106, 124, 134, 145, 169, 177, 187, 228, 243
job-specific 70
  job-specific proficiency 70

INDEX

job-specific proficiency thresholds 70
just-in-time 11
   just-in-time learning 11
   just-in-time learning opportunities 11

K

Key performance indicators (see: KPIs)
know-how 182, 194, 239
knowledge 3, 19, 22, 47, 59, 62, 75, 91, 123, 136, 169, 171, 177, 182, 183, 185–87, 189, 194–97, 220, 234, 239–41, 243
knowledgebase 239
KPIs 19, 26, 49–51, 53, 57, 72, 73, 94, 95, 101, 107, 109, 110, 147, 148, 165

L

large-scale 221
leader 13, 21–25, 30–32, 37, 38, 40, 47, 49, 55, 58, 59, 72–74, 84, 93, 94, 105, 163, 177, 180, 191, 197, 210, 242, 243
leaderboards 5, 175
leadership 20–22, 32, 40, 47, 55–57, 62, 63, 70, 73, 75, 95, 112, 125, 138, 152, 209, 212
   leadership for learning 40
   leadership for learning technology 40
   leadership framework 55, 56, 70, 75, 95, 112, 125, 138, 152
   leadership investment 73
   leadership strategies 62
   leadership thinking 209
learners 3, 5–9, 11–13, 35, 36, 75, 123, 133–37, 169–71, 174, 176, 186, 187, 199–201, 220, 228, 230, 232, 234–37
learning 3–13, 19–25, 34–36, 38–40, 47–49, 52, 53, 55, 56, 61–63, 67, 69–75, 88, 111, 112, 120, 122, 125, 131–38, 145, 151, 152, 159–62, 164, 166–78, 180, 182–84, 186, 187, 190, 192, 196, 197, 199–201, 207, 208, 210–12, 217–19, 221, 222, 231, 232, 234, 236
learning activities 12, 186, 199
learning analytics 3, 21, 161, 162, 164, 166, 221
learning app 175
learning approach 231
learning avenues 135
learning content 8, 136, 170, 177, 200, 219–21, 223
learning curve 136, 192
learning delivery 7, 168, 169, 174, 180
learning designers 4, 190
learning effectiveness 136
learning endeavors 20, 177
learning examples 171
learning experience 3–6, 9–11, 48, 49, 135, 136, 168, 169, 174–76, 199, 201, 232
learning goals 135, 222
learning industries 3
learning infrastructure 4
learning initiatives 21, 22
learning interventions 62
learning leaders 49
learning management 4
learning management systems (see: LMSs)
learning material 5, 172, 186, 200
learning-related 22
leverage 8, 20, 59, 111, 193, 195, 199, 207–9, 230, 232
LMSs 4, 112, 168, 197
low-frequency 123

INDEX

low-frequency events 123

M

management 4, 32, 53, 73, 82, 86, 93, 109–11, 145–47, 161, 162, 185–87, 194, 198, 210, 218
   management science 110
   management software 146
   management systems 4, 93, 185–87
   management tools 147, 185
manager 24, 32, 57–61, 63, 64, 92, 94, 95, 108, 111, 151, 177, 180, 239
manager-centric 64
managerial 31, 111
mapping 83, 95
mastery 30, 81, 108, 112, 134, 137, 149
measurable 105, 107
   measurable business outcomes 105
   measurable business results 107
measurement 39, 49, 56, 84, 105, 106, 109, 111, 149–52, 212
   measurement approach 109
   measurement mechanisms 150
   measurement technologies 109
measurement tool 39
mechanism 8, 50, 66, 112, 150, 151, 159, 170, 225
mentor 49, 57, 58, 60, 61, 63, 137, 165, 237
mentoring 3, 48, 49, 137, 159, 169, 170, 178, 236
mentor ratings 165
mentorship (see: mentoring)
messaging 198
metaverse 7, 11, 218
metrics 22–25, 28–31, 33, 37, 39, 50, 51, 54–56, 64–72, 86, 95, 101–7, 109–11, 120, 121, 145, 147, 149, 150, 159, 162, 163, 165–67, 211
microlearning 8, 11, 171, 175
mistakes 34, 36, 176, 200, 240
ML-based 168
   ML-based adaptive systems 168
m-learning (see: mobile - mobile learning)
mobile 5, 74, 168, 170, 171, 177, 180, 191, 199
   mobile applications 177
   mobile apps 5, 171, 180, 191, 199
   mobile devices 5
   mobile learning 5, 74, 168, 170, 171
   mobile learning technologies 168, 171
   mobile phones 5
mobile-enabled 187
module 8, 10, 11, 134, 136, 137, 164, 171, 175, 186, 222, 225, 229
monitoring 66, 73, 84, 146
multichannel 180, 191, 192, 197, 198
   multichannel communication 198
   multichannel communication tools 198
   multichannel communicator 180, 192, 197, 198
multiple 10, 19, 108, 151, 161, 181, 189, 197, 222, 232
   multiple aspects 19
   multiple channels 197
   multiple-choice 171, 229
   multiple coaches 189
   multiple discussions 222
   multiple levels 151
   multiple sources 181
   multiple technologies 108
multisensory 9, 11
multitask 90

INDEX

N

nanolearning 11
near-life experience 134
non-proficiency 36
non-technical 31

O

objectives 21, 22, 73, 92, 108, 111, 221
observation 120, 149, 191
obsolescence 20, 33, 73
onboarding 25, 29, 150, 164, 175, 184
on-demand 74, 135, 168, 171, 180, 187, 237
    on-demand informational content 187
    on-demand online learning 168
    on-demand performance technologies 74
    on-demand self-guided training 135
    on-demand videos 180
one-size-fits-all 48
online 3–5, 8, 112, 168, 169, 176, 177, 186, 187, 190, 196, 219, 232, 244
    online access 187
    online course 4, 5, 244
    online environment 4, 196
    online game-based learning 112
    online learners 176
    online learning 3, 4, 8, 168, 169, 176, 177, 186, 190, 232
    online learning content 177
    online learning platforms 186
    online or offline training 219
    online proctoring 8
    online searchable content 186
    online training (see: online - online learning)

online training material 232
online training simulations 176
on-the-job 26, 29, 101, 136, 165, 177
    on-the-job assignments 136
    on-the-job performance 101
    on-the-job proficiency 177
    on-the-job support 26, 165
    on-the-job training 29
operations 19, 20, 53, 62, 74, 82, 111, 123, 166, 185, 225
organization 21–24, 28, 34, 48–52, 54, 61, 63, 72–75, 85, 88, 92–94, 101–3, 105, 108–11, 137, 147, 150, 151, 161, 162, 166, 180, 192, 197, 198, 207–10, 239, 240
organizational 13, 20, 30, 47, 49, 59, 62–64, 72, 74, 108, 151, 159, 177, 186, 194, 243
    organizational competitiveness 13
    organizational context 30
    organizational culture 64
    organizational decision-making 49
    organizational design 62
    organizational goals 74
    organizational knowledge 59, 243
    organizational learning 20, 177, 186
    organizational levels 47, 151
    organizational performance 108
    organizational speed 72
    organizational strategy 63
    organizational structures 194
organization-wide 151
outcome 9, 22, 24, 26, 29, 37, 57, 69, 72, 84, 85, 93, 105–12, 120, 121, 125, 136, 138, 150, 162, 171, 172, 190, 192, 201
outcomes-related 106

P

pace 20, 34, 137, 178, 186

INDEX

pandemic 7, 19, 20, 28, 32, 35, 54, 133, 169, 177
parameter 52, 81, 82, 88, 131, 147, 181
participation 174, 175
pathways 6
performance 3, 4, 6, 19, 21, 25, 26, 29–31, 34–36, 38, 40, 49, 53–55, 57–61, 67, 72, 74, 81, 82, 84–91, 101, 103, 105–8, 110, 111, 123, 124, 132, 136, 137, 146, 159, 160, 162, 164, 165, 167, 171, 176, 177, 181, 183, 184, 190, 197, 209, 219–22, 236
  performance environment 58, 60
  performance gaps 222
  performance goals 59
  performance improvement 3, 25
  performance indicators (see: KPIs)
  performance issues 34
  performance level 26
  performance management 146, 162
  performance measure 26
  performance metrics 86, 101, 159
  performance objectives 108
  performance rating 90, 164, 165
  performance reviews 111
  performance specs 107
  performance stage 26
  performance standards 30, 38
  performance support 3, 61, 159, 160, 171, 183, 184, 190, 236
  performance support systems (see: PSSs)
  performance support technologies 159, 171, 183
  performance support tool 184
  performance system 108
  performance technologies 74, 184
  performance thresholds 26
  performance tracking 4
  performance training 108
performer 26, 57–61, 63, 70, 82–87, 91, 107, 167, 195–97
platform 3–6, 11, 12, 19, 22, 52, 58, 72, 74, 75, 86–88, 90, 92, 108, 111, 112, 132, 135, 169, 170, 173, 175, 180, 186–88, 191–93, 196–201
post-COVID 10, 35
post-hiring 93, 94
post-pandemic 60, 191
post-training 112
pre-assessment 136
pre-trained 239
problem-solving 9, 12, 91, 228
procedure 82, 83, 173, 239–42
productivity 23, 30, 38, 39, 48, 49, 82–85, 87, 101, 107, 109, 110, 123, 146, 150, 162, 185, 192, 193, 197, 208, 209
  productivity analysis 146
  productivity data 123
  productivity improvement 39
  productivity monitoring 84
  productivity term 30
professional 8, 11, 12, 23, 47, 73, 74, 85, 151, 189, 219, 220, 223, 228, 233, 237, 243
  professional content 233
  professional services 189
proficiency 23, 24, 26–32, 37, 48, 49, 54, 55, 57, 61, 64–71, 81, 91, 93, 95, 101–9, 111, 112, 119–21, 123, 125, 131, 132, 136, 138, 145, 147, 150, 151, 163, 165, 167, 170, 177, 178, 186, 187, 197, 199, 208, 209, 211
  proficiency definitions 102
  proficiency journey 61, 119, 163
  proficiency measure 64, 105–7, 147
  proficiency measurement 105, 109, 111

INDEX

proficiency metrics 64–69, 95, 102–6, 111, 120, 121, 145, 167, 211
proficiency scores 108
proficiency stage 165
proficiency threshold 68, 70, 101, 112, 119, 125, 138
proficiency trajectory 93
proficient 26, 31, 33, 34, 36–38, 88, 101, 102, 107, 112, 122, 123, 148, 150, 151, 187, 190
profile 50, 51, 81, 83–85, 89, 90, 92, 93, 119, 135–37, 163, 164, 195
progression 3, 26, 134, 226, 237
project-driven 193
PSSs 3, 59, 61, 62, 123, 124, 133–35, 152, 160, 171, 172, 177–80, 184, 186, 187, 190, 197, 236
purpose-driven 196, 197

Q

qualitative 24, 167, 180, 220, 234
quantifiable 64, 106, 110, 150, 151
   quantifiable measures 150, 151
   quantifiable metrics 64
quantitative (see: quantifiable)
quizzes 5, 112, 171, 217, 223, 229, 231

R

rapid 20, 34, 178
rating 54, 90, 134, 137, 164, 165, 195
readiness 34, 36–38, 150, 178
real-life 173–75
   real-life experiences 174
   real-life scenarios 173, 175
real-time 10, 52, 146, 181, 184, 188, 189, 191–93, 200, 201
   real-time alerts 146
   real-time collaboration 192, 193

real-time collaboration tools 192
real-time community 191
real-time conversations 189, 200
real-time data 181
real-time data insights 181
real-time data visualizations 181
real-time face-to-face meetings 193
real-time feedback 10, 52, 201
real-time feedback systems 52
real-time information 184
real-time insights 181
real-time support 188
real-time text communication 193
real-time work 193
real-world 9, 11
reduction 36, 39, 65, 66, 82
reflections 14, 41, 76, 96, 114, 126, 139, 153, 211
relationship 37, 59, 86–88, 109
remote 7, 8, 19, 62, 169, 173, 189, 193, 225, 232
remote-assisted 190
repository 180, 182, 183, 185, 194, 228, 231, 240, 241
requirement 21, 47, 82, 85, 89, 90, 168, 190
research 23, 31, 33, 38, 49, 57, 61, 66, 73, 74, 105, 120, 121, 133, 150, 168, 178, 189
researchers 74, 86
resources 5, 49, 54, 59, 66, 75, 89, 133, 136, 137, 159, 161, 169, 176–78, 185, 186, 201, 232, 241
results 64, 84, 88, 107, 109, 110, 119, 134, 178, 182, 183, 194–96, 242
role 12, 24–30, 47, 54, 64, 68, 70, 81, 91–93, 95, 105, 109, 110, 112, 131, 145, 151, 164, 166, 169, 178, 194, 218, 223, 233, 235, 236
rule-based 169, 217
rule-based AI 217

275

INDEX

rule-based AI systems 217

S

satisfaction 38, 54, 85, 87, 91, 93, 94, 104, 106, 107, 165, 201
scalability 19, 23
scalability-related 24
scenario-based 186, 228
scenario-based questions 186
scenarios 9, 11, 173–75, 228, 229
scientific 31, 176
scorecard 103
security 9, 10, 19, 53, 243
self-assessment 112, 180
self-leadership 86
self-learning 112, 232, 234
   self-learning mode 112
   self-learning video 232, 234
self-paced 170, 180, 186, 231, 232, 244
   self-paced content 180, 231
   self-paced learning 170, 186, 232
   self-paced learning activities 186
   self-paced learning technologies 170
   self-paced learning video 232
   self-paced material 231
   self-paced online course 244
service 31, 32, 34, 35, 52–54, 57, 81, 86, 90, 91, 103, 104, 106, 110, 124, 159, 164, 181, 184, 185, 187, 189, 198, 240
   service engineers 184
   service environments 184
   service executives 106
   service helpdesk 31
   service metrics 54
   service operations 185
   service profit 103, 104
   service representatives 86
   service roles 90
   service skills 91
   service staff 185
shorten 29, 33, 35, 36, 38–40, 53, 56, 61, 65, 69, 75, 81, 94, 95, 110, 123, 124, 133, 134, 136, 145, 148, 150, 151, 159, 168, 169, 174, 177, 184, 189, 192, 194, 199
   shortening of TTP 53
   shortening TTP 29, 33, 35, 36, 39, 40, 53, 56, 81, 94, 95, 134, 148, 150, 159, 168, 177, 184, 189, 192
   shorten the curve 169
   shorten the learning curve 136
   shorten the time-to-market 35
simulated 106, 108, 112, 134
   simulated assessments 112
   simulated experience 134
   simulated performance 108
simulation 5, 11, 12, 49, 52, 108, 112, 171, 173, 176
   simulation training 52
   simulation training tools 52
simulator testing 108
skilled 92, 138, 168
skill-related 33, 34
skills 3, 12, 21, 22, 24, 28, 29, 31–35, 37, 38, 47, 50, 51, 67–71, 75, 81–84, 90–94, 107, 111, 113, 119, 120, 122–25, 131, 133, 135–37, 150, 167, 169, 171, 174, 186, 187, 190, 194, 195, 200, 209, 211, 220, 221, 228
skillsets 84
software 3, 4, 7, 19, 52, 55, 84, 90, 110, 134, 146, 177, 180, 181, 185, 187–89, 196, 231
software-driven 11
speed-centric 64
   speed-centric ecosystem 64
speed-enabling 55, 56
   speed-enabling ecosystem 55, 56
speed-focused 66
   speed-focused strategies 66

INDEX

speed-savvy 62
speed-savvy leadership 62
speed-to-proficiency 36, 37, 52, 61, 62, 167
stakeholders 192, 222
statistical 88
step-by-step 172, 184, 185, 220
story-based 228, 229
storyboard 225, 231
strategic 13, 19–22, 32, 39, 40, 47, 55, 56, 59, 61, 70–75, 95, 102, 104, 112, 125, 138, 151, 152, 162, 167, 209, 210, 212
   strategic behaviors 59
   strategic focus 61, 151
   strategic framework 39
   strategic function 20
   strategic leaders 13
   strategic leadership 22, 40, 95, 112, 125, 138, 152, 209
   strategic learning 21, 40, 55, 56, 72, 73, 210, 212
   strategic management 32
   strategic objectives 21
   strategic organization 102
   strategic plans 210
   strategic questions 167
   strategic success 22
   strategic technology 47, 55, 56, 70, 71, 210
   strategic thinking 20, 21, 72, 73
   strategic viewpoint 19, 21
strategically 20, 54, 60, 103, 120, 125, 177, 178, 185, 192, 199, 242
strategist 39, 217
strategy 21, 22, 39, 47, 54, 55, 62–64, 66, 67, 69, 70, 72, 75, 81, 85–87, 95, 101, 103, 108, 112, 123, 125, 132, 138, 145, 152, 160, 166, 167, 186, 190–92, 199, 207, 209–12
supervision 26
supervisor 106, 107, 112

systematic 219, 230, 241
systems 3, 4, 7, 9, 39, 51, 52, 55, 56, 58–61, 66, 82, 93, 106, 108–11, 124, 136, 137, 145, 149–51, 160, 168, 169, 180, 181, 185–87, 189, 198, 200, 207–9, 217, 221, 236

T

taxonomy 194, 195
teachable 177
teaching 3, 7, 159, 169, 172, 176, 182, 200
   teaching AI 182
   teaching aid 172
   teaching methods 176, 200
   teaching technologies 169
technology 56
technology leadership 56
technological 6, 8, 20, 21, 23, 24, 39, 40, 48, 49, 62, 159, 176, 183
   technological advancements 6
   technological advances 176
   technological challenges 8
   technological changes 21
   technological implementation 49
   technological infrastructure 24, 183
   technological innovation 20
   technological needs 20
   technological requirements 21
   technological revolution 62
   technological solutions 23, 48
   technological thinking 159
   technological thinking process 159
technologist 20, 23, 47, 61, 145, 151, 178, 182, 190
technology 3–6, 8–13, 19–25, 28, 34, 38–40, 47–49, 51–61, 64, 67–75, 81, 83–85, 87–90, 92–95, 101, 102, 106, 108–12, 119, 120, 124, 125, 131–38, 145, 148, 149, 151,

INDEX

152, 159, 160, 163, 166–78, 180, 183–87, 189–94, 196–98, 201, 207–10, 212, 217, 242
technology company 51, 55, 88
technology department 166
technology effectiveness 23
technology group 169
technology implementation 23, 24, 40, 47, 70, 75, 207
technology infrastructure 25
technology initiatives 72
technology investments 74
technology landscapes 47
technology leader 21–25, 40, 55, 72, 73, 210
technology leadership 21, 47, 55, 56, 70, 212
technology needs 48, 209
technology pre-implementation 22
technology procurement 194
technology projects 22
technology selection 25
technology strategist 39, 217
technology strategy 21, 75, 160, 186
technology systems 56
technology thinking 55, 56, 71
technology thinking framework 71
technology-centric 64
technology-driven 20
tech-savvy 48, 59, 209
thinking-intensive 228, 230
three-dimensional 6
time-related 33
time-saver 217
timestamps 149
time-to-activity 148
time-to-certification 150
time-to-closure 147, 148
time-to-market 33–36, 72
time-to-productivity 84, 150, 166
time-to-proficiency 25, 27, 29, 65, 210
time-to-readiness 61, 135
time-tracking 145–47
trainers 136, 189, 237, 243
training 3, 4, 8, 9, 13, 21, 23–25, 29–34, 36, 37, 39, 47, 51, 52, 61, 62, 83, 86–88, 92, 94, 108, 112, 120, 122, 124, 125, 131, 133–38, 159, 163–65, 167–70, 173–78, 184–90, 193, 196, 217–26, 229–32, 235–37, 239, 240, 242
training business 21
training capacity 135
training cases 31
training classes 196, 225
training content (see: learning - learning content)
training costs 165
training courses 225, 229, 239
training data 164
training delivery (see: learning - learning delivery)
training designers (see: learning - learning designers)
training development 217, 219, 220, 222, 242
training duration 23, 33, 36, 39
training event 177, 190
training gap 222
training hours 88
training intervention 185–87
training material 219, 221, 231, 232
training modules 136, 164, 175, 186, 229
training need 219–21
training outline 224
training program 4, 29, 30, 86, 88, 125, 137, 163, 218–20, 230–32
training projects 218
training records 164, 165
training requirement 190

INDEX

training sessions 8
training simulations 176
training specialists 220
training strategies 87
training structure 220
training technologies 135, 159, 169, 170
training video 218, 219
transform 7, 9, 85, 185, 199
transformation 25, 64, 94
troubleshoot 184, 189, 193, 228, 229
TTP (see: time-to-proficiency)
tutoring 9
tutors 201

U

unproductive 82
upgrading 20, 73
upskilling 124
up-to-date 21, 73, 74, 194

V

valuable 21, 86, 136, 176, 240, 242
    valuable feedback 176
    valuable insights 21, 86, 136, 240
    valuable tool 242
virtual 4, 6–8, 11, 12, 90, 135, 169, 172–74, 176
    virtual classroom 4
    virtual classrooms 4, 11
    virtual environment 11
    virtual learning 7, 8, 169
    virtual learning delivery (see: virtual - virtual training delivery)
    virtual learning platforms 169
    virtual mode 169
    virtual reality 6
    virtual simulations 11
    virtual situation 176
    virtual team projects 12

virtual training 8, 135, 169
virtual training delivery 7, 169
virtual training sessions 8
virtual training technologies 135
virtual world 172–74
visualization 86, 147, 180, 181, 218
    visualization platform 180
    visualization tools 180
VR (see: virtual reality)

W

workflow 62, 170, 178, 184, 190, 192, 208, 237
    workflow-based 133, 134, 236
workforce 24, 32–37, 40, 50, 51, 53, 55, 83, 84, 87, 89, 92, 93, 111, 124, 125, 138, 145, 159–62, 166, 170, 178, 207–9
    workforce analytics 84, 124, 159–62, 166, 170
    workforce capabilities 208
    workforce data 89, 92, 125
    workforce decisions 162
    workforce learning 178
    workforce management 93, 145, 162
    workforce needs 24
    workforce productivity 162
    workforce readiness 36
    workforce skills 34, 209
workplace 12, 20, 24, 33, 35, 36, 38, 47, 88, 93, 146, 152, 159, 162, 163, 166, 167, 193
    workplace analytics 146, 152, 159, 162, 163, 166, 167
    workplace issues 162
    workplace learning 36, 38, 88
    workplace requirements 47

X

INDEX

xlookup 220, 221, 223, 225, 228, 229, 233–36, 239, 241
  xlookup course 223
  xlookup function 223, 228, 229, 233, 241

xlookup procedures 223

THE AUTHOR

Named as the Chief Learning Officer of the Year, Dr. Raman K. Attri is a sought-after coach to the futuristic CLOs. Dr. Attri is the world's leading authority on the "science of speed" in professional learning and performance, with over two decades of research in performance science. His outstanding achievements have earned him recognition as a Brainz Global 500 leader alongside other stellar personalities such as Oprah Winfrey, Gary Vee, Jim Kwik, and Jim Shetty. He has been inducted as one of the '50 under 50 Leaders' by the New York City Journal.

He is a multifaceted personality with a range of talents, including being a scientist, author, speaker, L&D leader, and artist. Despite being permanently disabled since childhood, Dr. Attri is known as a powerhouse of positivity and inspiration. He has transformed his inability to walk into a unique expertise in teaching people how to walk faster in their professional world.

He is the creator of a time-tested, proven system that can help leaders and organizations speed up the path to mastery and leadership in any domain by twofold. His most recent project is the

GetThereFaster portal, a comprehensive resource for anyone seeking to learn the secrets of learning better and faster.

Dr. Attri is a professional speaker who shares research-based insights at leading international conferences with top business executives, helping them to master speed in business, shorten workforce time-to-proficiency, and accelerate employee development.

He is also a global training thought leader at a Fortune 500 technology corporation, managing one of the world's top 10 Hall-of-Fame training organizations.

As a prolific author of 50 multi-genre books, Dr. Attri writes books and articles on various topics ranging from business and leadership to performance and expertise, as well as training and development to HR and workforce development.

Passionate about continuous learning, Dr. Attri has earned two doctorates in learning, over 100 international educational credentials, several degrees and diplomas, and some of the highest certifications. He is an authentic accelerated learning business coach who practices what he preaches.

Featured in over 200 articles, interviews, and shows, Dr. Attri was awarded as one of the Most Admired Global Indians of 2022. He is a highly sought-after expert whose remarkable achievements inspire everyone he touches to strive for true excellence in their personal and professional lives.

You may contact @DrRamanKAttri on social media platforms like Facebook, LinkedIn, and YouTube. Or visit https://get-there-faster.com to know more.

THE BOOK

Strategic Learning Technology Leadership is your guide to staying ahead of the curve in a landscape defined by rapid technological revolutions, including artificial intelligence. This book teaches visionary L&D architects how to be strategic about the latest generation of learning technologies. This book offers a groundbreaking exploration into leveraging cutting-edge learning technologies to propel your workforce into the future. Drawing from two decades of international research and real-world corporate leadership, this book is a roadmap to survive, thrive and accelerate in the AI era.

Through real-world examples and actionable insights, you'll discover how forward-thinking organizations are using state-of-the-art analytics and tools to accelerate workforce capabilities. From redefining business KPIs to harnessing the potential of time-to-proficiency metrics, from hiring to proficiency metrics, and from efficient learning paths to time measurements, each chapter is a masterclass in strategic technology leadership.

In this book, you will learn:

- Understand the strategic nature of learning technologies in speeding up employee learning, performance, and development.
- View time-to-proficiency metrics as an unmatchable competitive weapon in today's market.
- Leverage time-to-proficiency metrics as the KPIs for learning technology success.
- Assess how new and future technologies can help to accelerate workforce development rapidly.

- Adopt a strategic technology leadership thinking framework on implementing technologies to speed up employee development.
- Deep dive into five critical strategies to evaluate, select, and implement learning technologies toward reducing time-to-proficiency.
- Strategize the selection and use of workplace analytics and technologies.
- Drive strategic alignment of analytics and technologies with business outcomes.

This is not just any book on learning technologies. It is your one-stop guide to master the leadership thinking to assess, select, and implement technologies that not only improve efficiency but also drive competitive advantage.

Whether you're a seasoned HR leader, L&D think-tank, learning technologist, or corporate IT executive, this book is your call to rethink your leadership approaches and harness the power of the latest technologies to lead your organization into the future.

Do you want to be a speed-savvy CLO or Training Leader with an edge?

Find out about science-backed strategies and corporate training transformation with **GetThereFaster L&D Leaders Academy**. To match the speed with time, you need to master the art and science of speed. Learn the latest and greatest research-backed frameworks and models to accelerate your workforce's performance ahead of time. Develop your managers to stay prepared for the era of AI. Reach out today for a no-obligation call to discuss a Chief Learning Officers' workshop or learning executive coaching session. Book Dr Raman K Attri and get coached by a leading expert on the science of organizational learning speed.

Becoming a top L&D thought Leader in the era of speed has never been this fast!!

Email: contact@get-there-faster.com
Socials: https://nue.bio/chief
Website: https://get-there-faster.com

www.ingramcontent.com/pod-product-compliance
Lightning Source LLC
LaVergne TN
LVHW061540070526
838199LV00077B/6848